Business Architecture

To Lindsay and Lizzie

JW

To Jasmine, Nicholas, Arthur and Alessandra

GM

Business Architecture

A Practical Guide

JONATHAN WHELAN and
GRAHAM MEADEN

GOWER

Published by
Gower Publishing Limited
Wey Court East
Union Road
Farnham
Surrey, GU9 7PT
England

Gower Publishing Company
110 Cherry Street
Suite 3-1
Burlington,
VT 05401-3818
USA

www.gowerpublishing.com

British Library Cataloguing in Publication Data
Whelan, Jonathan.
    Business architecture : a practical guide.
    1. Industrial organization. 2. Industrial efficiency – Management. 3. Organizational effectiveness – Management.
    I. Title II. Meaden, Graham.
    658.1–dc23

Library of Congress Cataloging-in-Publication Data
Whelan, Jonathan.
    Business architecture : a practical guide / by Jonathan Whelan and Graham Meaden.
        p. cm.
    Includes bibliographical references and index.
    ISBN 978-1-4094-3859-5 (alk. paper) – ISBN 978-1-4094-3860-1 (ebook)
  1. Strategic planning. 2. Organization. 3. Management. I. Meaden, Graham. II. Title.

    HD30.28.M415 2011
    658.4'012–dc23

                                                                        2011052065

ISBN 9781409438595 (hbk)
ISBN 9781409438601 (ebk)

Printed in the United Kingdom by Henry Ling Limited,
at the Dorset Press, Dorchester, DT1 1HD

Contents

List of Figures

List of Tables

About the Authors

Jonathan Whelan

Jonathan is an established business architect who has over 25 years' experience in a variety of change-related roles within leading organizations. A broad spectrum of businesses have benefited from his observations, and a number of his insights have led to significant programmes of work within corporate organizations. Jonathan has given specific consideration to the significance of technology to businesses and in particular the opportunities and issues that face business users of technology. In recent years his focus has been exclusively on business architecture, and in particular the formulation of business architecture for global institutions from a strategic level through to implementation at a programme and project level.

As well as having considerable practical experience, Jonathan is a Chartered Engineer and a Fellow of the British Computer Society. He is also TOGAF® 9-certified and Zachman-certified.

In his spare time, Jonathan writes on business technology issues and opportunities. He is the author of numerous books, including *email@work* (2000) and *e-Business Matters* (2000), and he has also contributed to numerous professional, trade and national press publications. His books have received wide acclaim from government and professional organizations and senior business executives.

Graham Meaden

Graham started his career 25 years ago in software development and systems architecture. Most notably, he was the architect for the contactless smartcard system Oyster Card® that is used to manage access and fare collection in London's public transport system.

Since then, Graham has been a practising enterprise architect, as a consultant and member of staff, in the banking, insurance, government, transportation and energy industry sectors. In recent years he has focused on business architecture and setting up architecture practices. Most recently, as part of heading up the global Strategic Architecture and Business Architecture teams for HSBC Group, he defined the standards for the bank's global Business Process Management centre of excellence. Along the way he has made extensive use of enterprise architecture frameworks and he has contributed, along with others, in the development of TOGAF® 9.

After brief spells in Asia and North America, Graham is now based in the UK. He continues to provide business architecture consultancy, mentoring and coaching and is also a certified Managing Successful Programmes practitioner.

Foreword

I love this book. I have read it two times, and I am looking forward to reading it again!

Yes, I know Graham Meaden and Jonathan Whelan, and you could surmise that I am simply biased. However, my bias has nothing to do with why I loved the book. It is a great book. It is a book whose time has come. The world needs this book at this important time.

A lot of material has been written about business architecture (by some definition), going back to *The Principles of Scientific Management* (1911) by Frederick Taylor. A lot of people talk about business architecture – at least going back to 1989, in my own experience, a US National Institute of Science and Technology research project, the origins of the FEA Framework and an early publication of my Framework (The Zachman Framework). A lot of people define business architecture differently (I know a lot of people who have a lot of different opinions and definitions for business architecture). Not too many people *do* business architecture, at least not in a comprehensive and definitive fashion (in my estimation).

Clearly, the time has come for *Business Architecture: A Practical Guide* (see my observations below).

One reason why I like this book is that it tells it like it is.

A lot of people forget (or don't like to think about the fact) that an enterprise is the most complex creation of which humanity has yet conceived. And the enterprise doesn't have to get very big to be very complex – a subject that Graham and Jonathan address specifically. (I like to use the word 'enterprise' as an encompassing idea that contextualizes its business architecture.)

The characteristics of the Information Age that are universally recognized are extreme complexity and extreme change. The analytical approach to accommodate complexity is classification. You have to get all of the like things into one category in order to understand their characteristics and then examine the relationships between the categories to express complexity. Graham and Jonathan structure the book conveniently into categories to convey the complexity of business architecture in a comprehensible fashion.

The complexity lies in the relationships between the simple, understandable categories, and the change, the dynamics, lies in the variability of the relationships. How better to express the complexity and change than in matrices, the relationships between two categories? I like the book's matrices. They can be very definitive and can very simply depict extreme complexity.

Another reason I like the book is their extensive use of metaphors and examples. The only way I can understand concepts that have little or no precedent is to relate them to something I know – a metaphor. I like the physical world of tangible objects that I live in or fly over or ride in. These are understandable as a conceptual basis for understanding something unknown. Where the metaphor doesn't hold, a good example from real business life is very helpful. The book's metaphors and examples are really helpful in communicating these rather arcane business architecture concepts.

I like their acknowledgement that there are short-term issues, and there are long-term issues. A lot of material has been developed to address the business's short-term issues. This is the way to produce immediate, measurable results – benefits that those of us in the Western world especially appreciate.

In the 24 July 2006 *Fortune Magazine* article 'The New Rules', the author, Betsy Morris, observes that Jack Welch, the retired CEO of General Electric, is held up as the epitome of the modern CEO: 'Jack's Rules are now the business equivalent of the holy writ, bedrock wisdom that has been open to interpretation, perhaps, but not dispute.'

The article continues with the theme that 'Jack's rules' are 'the old rules'. It also quotes Harvard Business School's Rakesh Khurana in observing that 'Managing to create shareholder value became managed earnings became managing quarter by quarter to please the street.' 'That meant a disinvestment in the future,' says Khurana. 'It was a reversal of everything that made capitalism the envy of the rest of the world: the willingness of a CEO to forgo dividends and make an investment that wouldn't be realized until one or two CEO's down the road. Now we are at a hinge point in American capitalism.'

Yes, we are! How do we intend to accommodate orders of magnitude increases in complexity and orders of magnitude increases in the rate of change? If you read newspapers or watch TV, you are acutely aware of current evidence that enterprises of today, in both public and private sectors, are not accommodating extreme complexity and extreme change. We are not talking about some day in the 'sweet by and by'.

Enter business architecture!

My observation is: you cannot simply focus on short-term issues to the exclusion of the long term! You are optimizing the parts and sub-optimizing the whole. And at the point in time when you need to have your business architecture in order to address the increasing plethora of non-deterministic challenges and escalating complexity – it is too late!

I have spent most of my professional life trying to understand and classify the total set of things that exist that are relevant and that can be formalized, made explicit, that would constitute the total knowledgebase of the enterprise – everything that could be known to create, change, manage, operate an enterprise, to enable an enterprise to be viable in an extremely complex and dynamic environment – the Information Age. That is, my Framework is an 'ontology' – it is not a methodology. I like Graham and Jonathan's characterization of my Framework in the book.

I spent my life trying to understand the templates, the meta model, the ontology for describing an enterprise, because until you have an ontology, nothing is repeatable and nothing is predictable. I know very little about the actual contents, the population of the templates. That is another *big* reason why I love this book. Graham and Jonathan have given me a great appreciation for what the actual contents, descriptive representations, of the enterprise would contain. This is the reason why I am going to read this book a third and a fourth – and maybe many more times!

Now here, in my opinion, is the most practical message of the book, found early on:

> *The delivery of an architecture doesn't bring any direct benefit in its own right. Business architecture is not a solution, it is a tool. In the right hands it becomes an asset of strategic value to the organization.*

If business architecture becomes a solution, it is only good for one point in time. If it is a tool, it is the most valuable asset the enterprise owns – the knowledgebase of the enterprise that accommodates extreme complexity and forms the basis for change. That is what is needed to survive in the Information Age. If you have no idea how something works at the level of definition required to make actual changes to it, what are you going to change and how are you going to change it? 'In the right hands [business architecture] becomes an asset of strategic value to the organization.'

I hope every business architect reads this book. In fact, I hope that every CEO who so enjoys Jack Welch's books will read this book! To repeat the quote from Rakesh Khurana, whatever happened to 'the willingness of a CEO to forgo dividends and make an investment that wouldn't be realized until one or two CEOs down the road'?

This is not to say there are no benefits to be realized from business architecture in the short term – there are plenty of benefits. But somebody better start thinking about business architecture as a tool for the future, or there is not likely to be a future!

Business Architecture: A Practical Guide – the time has come.

Thank you, Graham and Jonathan.

John A. Zachman
Glendale, California

Preface

Introducing Business Architecture

Organizations today exist in an environment of unprecedented change, and they do so against a backdrop of a global, competitive marketplace, the fast-paced enablement of technology, amplified regulation and ever-increasing organizational complexity. It is these dynamics that are leading organizations to recognize and embrace business architecture.

The intent of business architecture is not new: it is to enable organizations to achieve their business plans; to realize their vision. But what role does business architecture play? What unique value proposition does business architecture bring to the table? For business architects to get a seat at the table there need to be clear and consistent answers to these questions – there needs to be a compelling value proposition.

However, business architecture can be a difficult 'sell' – it is often perceived to be abstract and lacking in tangible delivery. To succeed, business architecture must be pragmatic, and to be sustainable, it must focus on driving out value while recognizing that the value may not be immediate.

Business architecture:

- provides a way to describe and visualize the components of an organization;

- enables organizations to be viewed holistically, providing traceability from intent (investment of financial and human capital) to outcome (operational cost reduction, faster time to market, reduced cost-to-market and cost-in-market, customer satisfaction, shareholder satisfaction and so on);

- provides a mechanism to balance risk with opportunity;

- is a collection of assets, methods, processes, directives and resources that combine to realize a purpose, a goal, a vision;

- is complementary to other disciplines (such as P3M, business strategy and enterprise architecture).

Business architecture is not 'the solution'. If it is well-defined and shrewdly executed, it is a valuable asset, but if it is poorly defined and carelessly executed, it is a liability.

We do not believe there is any competing alternate term for business architecture. The only term that may conflict or confuse is enterprise architecture (EA). What is the relationship between enterprise architecture and business architecture? Does business architecture sit within enterprise architecture, or vice versa? With this book we hope to advance the importance and scope of business architecture beyond what it is described as within current EA frameworks and standards.

About this Book

This book promotes the use and evolution of practices that are tried and tested; they may not be perfect – few things are. It recognizes and promotes the use of materials and methods that already exist; many organizations and many people (and not just business architects) have invested a significant amount of time in establishing a pool of knowledge and experience. Diversity of background, context and challenge is driving out many niche techniques and methods that will ultimately contribute to this evolving practice.

This book does not propose a revolutionary way of structuring, developing or practising business architecture. Nor does it recommend a new definition for business architecture or a new notation to be adopted; there are plenty of definitions and notations out there already. This book is intended to be what it says: a practical guide that focuses on the most important aspects of business architecture – those that are crucial to delivering value.

Business architecture should not be practised in isolation, nor should it be thought of as a one-off process; it needs to be woven into the fabric of the organization. And so we illustrate the opportunities for weaving the business architecture practice into this fabric through the various stakeholders and life cycles that exist, either formally or informally, within an organization.

Alongside acknowledging best practice, this book explores a new, inspirational level of business architecture while recognizing that the best way to realize the vision is one step at a time.

This book:

- sets out the need for business architecture and the value that can be derived from it;

- identifies the relationship between business architecture, its stakeholders and the disciplines related to it (for example, business strategy and planning);

- describes the levels within organizations at which business architecture can be applied and the types of products that it delivers;

- discusses the core elements (or building blocks) of business architecture – the foundations on which to build a business architecture;

- highlights the practical aspects of establishing a credible business architecture practice, including the critical success factors and the competencies required of a business architect;

- identifies the resources (materials, tools and methods) that exist to inform, enrich and enable a business architecture capability.

Organizations are becoming too complex to evolve without a plan of the agents of which they are comprised. Without business architecture, organizations may be left in the dark as to the real operational risks they face, and the flexibility and agility that they should exhibit. The risks are there; they may be hidden or not easily visible, but they are there. It is how those risks are managed that can determine survival, and beyond that, excellence.

Who Should Read this Book

This book will appeal to you if you are someone who:

- is pivotal to the success of investment and change in organizations;

- recognizes the need to link investment decisions to business strategy;

- is involved in innovation such as the development of new products, services or business propositions;

- interacts with business architects and wants a greater appreciation of business architecture;

- is a practising business architect wishing to evolve their own architectures and practices;

- is part of an architecture practice that is struggling to gain traction and/or is looking to make improvements;

- is having to justify the establishment of a business architecture practice;

- has heard about business architecture and wants to understand more about it;

- is embarking on a career as a business architect;

- is in education and is considering business architecture (or a related disciplines) as a career;

- is enrolled on a graduate or post-graduate course of Business Administration and wishes to understand how business architecture relates.

Business architecture is an industry-independent discipline, so it will appeal to a broad spectrum of people.

How this Book is Organized

We have divided the book into six parts, as shown in Figure 0.1. These parts are based on the layers of the business architecture Value Creation Model (VCM) that we introduce in Chapter 1. As well as forming the backbone of the book, the model provides an overall structure for describing the numerous layers of business architecture.

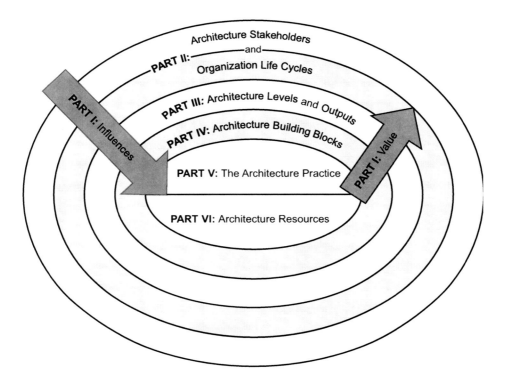

Figure 0.1   How this book is organized

Each part is further divided in chapters. However, we recognize that not everyone will want to read this book from cover to cover, so we have structured each chapter so that it can be read as a stand-alone text.

The parts follow the introductory chapter (Chapter 1) and precede our vision for the future of business architecture in Chapter 18.

We recognize that what you want out of this book may well depend on your role, therefore in Table 0.1 we suggest some specific paths through the text depending on what it is.

We hope you get as much from reading this book as we did from writing it.

Table 0.1   Role-based paths through the text

Parts and Chapters Role	Part I					Part II		Part III		Part IV		Part V				Part VI		
	1	2	3	4	5	6	7	8	9	10	11	12	13	14	15	16	17	18
C-Suite: CEO, CFO, CIO etc.	×	×	×	×	×	×			×									×
Change agent: portfolio, programme, project manager etc.	×	×	×	×	×	×		×	×									×
Architect: business, enterprise, capability etc.	×	×	×	×	×	×	×	×	×	×	×	×	×	×	×	×	×	×
Considering a career as a business architect	×		×		×							×	×					×
General reader	×	×	×	×	×	×			×									×

Acknowledgements

Much of the content of this book is based on our own experiences, but we have not been alone on our journey. We have learnt from working with many talented architects whose passion has been inspirational – you know who you are! – as well as the business executives, programme and project managers, and others who have given us the opportunity to practise and develop our trade.

Reviewing drafts of the book requires time and dedication, and we received these in abundance from our reviewers. Mark Carr, Serena Li and Peter Tapp gave detailed and supportive feedback of early drafts. We are also grateful to Sally Bean and Jeff Scott for their reviews of drafts and for sharing their insights in driving forward the adoption and future development of business architecture. We also acknowledge John Zachman, not only for his enthusiastic support of our efforts, but also for his contribution to the field of architecture over many years.

There are a number of companies and organizations which provided input and allowed us to use their material, including the BBC, Forrester, The Open Group, Wiley Inc. and Zachman International, Inc., and of course all the websites that we raided for information. In addition, we are grateful to Celestial Consulting and Selvyn Wright. We also recognize that technology has had a part to play (not least because we live almost 6,000 miles apart), especially Skype and Dropbox, both of which are underpinned by great business models.

We are indebted to Jonathan Norman, our publisher, for confirming that the market was missing a book such as ours. Also thanks to Jonathan's colleagues at Gower for their enthusiasm while carrying out the numerous activities that transformed our final draft into the finished article – these include Fiona Martin, Chris Muddiman, Emily Ruskell, Huw Jones, Sue White, Melisa Young and many others.

Writing a book invariably results in sacrifices, and it is usually those who are closest to the authors who make the greatest sacrifices and provide the greatest encouragement. This book is no exception, and so our greatest thanks go to Alessandra, a 'high five' to Arthur (who so often provided Skype interludes), and to Lindsay (not least of all for the proofreading), Lizzie (who 'encouraged' the venture in the first place) and Poppy (who, alas, received fewer walks than she would have liked).

Abbreviations

ACORD   Association for Cooperative Operations Research and Development

ADM   Architecture Development Method

APQC   American Productivity and Quality Center

BAD   Business Architecture Description

BSC   Balanced Scorecard

BMM   Business Motivation Model

BOM   Bill Of Materials

BPM   Business Process Management

BPMM   Business Process Maturity Model

BPMN   Business Process Model and Notation

BRM   Business Reference Model

CBA   Certified Business Architect

CBM   Component Business Model

CEO   Chief Executive Officer

CFO   Chief Financial Officer

CIO	Chief Information Officer
CMMI	Capability Maturity Model Integration
COBIT	Control Objectives for Information and related Technology
COO	Chief Operating Officer
CRM	Customer Relationship Management
CSF	Critical Success Factor
CTO	Chief Technology Officer
DODAF	Department Of Defense Architecture Framework
DRM	Data Reference Model
EA	Enterprise Architecture
EDAP	Environment, Direction, Action and Performance
EM BRM	Exploration and Mining Business Reference Model
EPC	Event-driven Process Chain
ERP	Enterprise Resource Planning
eTOM	enhanced Telecom Operations Map
FEA	Federal Enterprise Architecture
GERAM	Generalized Enterprise Reference Architecture and Methodology
IDEF	Integration Definition
IEEE	Institute of Electrical and Electronics Engineers
IT	Information Technology

ITIL®   Information Technology Infrastructure Library

KPI   Key Performance Indicator

LEED   Leadership in Energy and Environmental Design

MODAF   Ministry Of Defence Architecture Framework

MSP®   Managing Successful Programmes

NAFTA   North American Free Trade Agreement

NASCIO   National Association of State Chief Information Officers

NGOSS   New Generation Operations Systems and Software

OGC   Office of Government Commerce

PCF   Process Classification Framework

PEST   Political, Economic, Social, and Technological

PMBOK®   Project Management Body of Knowledge

PMI   Project Management Institute

PRM   Performance Reference Model

P3M   Portfolio, Programme and Project Management

RACI   Responsible, Accountable, Consulted, Informed

RASCI   Responsible, Accountable, Supporting, Consulted, Informed

RBM   Replicable Business Model

RFC   Request For Change

RFID   Radio Frequency Identifier

ROI   Return On Investment

RUP®   Rational Unified Process

SABSA   Sherwood Applied Business Security Architecture

SCOR®   Supply Chain Operations Reference

SFIA   Skills Framework for the Information Age

SIPOC   Supplier, Input, Process, Output, Customer

SLA   Service Level Agreement

SMART   Specific, Measurable, Achievable, Realistic, Time-bound

SPEM   Software and systems Process Engineering Metamodel
             specification

SRM   Service component Reference Model

STEER   Socio-cultural, Technological, Economic, Ecological, Regulatory

SWOT   Strengths, Weaknesses, Opportunities, Threats

TBM   Target Business Model

TCO   Total Cost of Ownership

TOGAF®   The Open Group Architecture Framework

TOM   Target Operating Model

UML   Unified Modelling Language

VCM   Value Creation Model

VRM   Value Reference Model

1

Introduction

The Macro Picture

The extraordinary events in the financial markets early in the twenty-first century had a substantial impact on the global economy – almost everyone was impacted in some way, either directly or indirectly. Private and public organizations tightened their belts, reignited their focus on delivering value from their investments and demanded more bang from their buck. But, as the saying goes, 'Money isn't everything,' and characteristics such as a compelling customer experience, innovation and agility have become prominent differentiators.

At the same time, organizations have become increasingly complex ecosystems. Rigid organization structures are being replaced with a network of inter-related, loosely coupled capabilities fused by a common vision – or at least you would hope so! Product and service offerings are now more sophisticated, and the 'customer expectation' bar is rising every day. Industries and marketplaces face increasing regulation, introducing constraints on the one hand, and opportunities on the other.

International companies, once 'holding companies' for a loose confederation of businesses operating in geographical silos, are now striving to become truly internationalized businesses. New technologies that enable the creation of a systems and informational platform capable of supporting global operations are now breaking down traditional silos and creating integrated businesses. The benefits of rationalization, economies of scale, global customer propositions, franchising and labour arbitrage are driving businesses to become webs of interconnected and integrated service providers in a way that they have never been before.

But that just brings us as far as today. What about the big issues that we face in the future? The growing global economy and globalization increases competition, and that in turn fuels greater innovation. The frequency and potency of technological innovation is likely to increase. Other dimensions also play their part: scarce resources (minerals, water and food) in the face of a growing human population. Ecological concerns are driving organizations to consider total product life cycle beyond sale into product recall and recycle. Demographics is forcing a greater focus on long-term financial planning and commitments. Trading zones and supranationalism are stimulating the free movement of labour and immigration, and social networking is enabling new kinds of democracy.

About Business Architecture

Against this backdrop of change, business architecture is maturing into a discipline in its own right, rising from the pool of inter-related practices that include business strategy, enterprise architecture, business portfolio planning and change management – to name but a few.

But what is business architecture? Ask ten architects and invariably you will get at least ten answers! It is different things to different people, although there is generally common ground about what it aims to achieve. There is no single agreed definition of business architecture, or any other architecture for that matter. We do not intend to offer yet another definition, although we do position ourselves to address this complex topic.

In this book, we view business architecture as a collection of assets, methods, processes and resources that all contribute towards enabling the goals of the organization. Of course, to existing practitioners there is more to it than that, and we address those details, including the purpose of business architecture, its value proposition and what the key assets of a business architecture look like.

Several definitions of business architecture exist:

- The Institute of Electrical and Electronics Engineers (IEEE)[1] defines architecture as:

---

1   IEEE Standard 1471-2000: *IEEE Recommended Practice for Architectural Description of Software-Intensive Systems.*

The fundamental organization of a system embodied in its components, their relationships to each other, and to the environment, and the principles guiding its design and evolution.

Although this is a definition for the architecture of software systems, the core concept is applicable to business architecture. You can replace 'system' with 'business'; the components are the resources (people, technologies, facilities and so on) that collaborate to deliver products and services.

- The Open Group Architecture Framework (TOGAF)[2] defines business architecture as:

a description of the structure and interaction between the business strategy, organization, functions, business processes, and information needs.

- The Business Architecture Special Interest Group[3] defines business architecture as:

a blueprint of the enterprise that provides a common understanding of the organization and is used to align strategic objectives and tactical demands.

- Wikipedia[4] defines business architecture as:

a part of an enterprise architecture related to corporate business, and the documents and diagrams that describe that architectural structure of business.

Each definition is valid, but no single definition is all-encompassing. In this book we aim to push the boundaries by exploring deeper into the discipline of business architecture, for example by addressing the non-deterministic, 'living' ecosystem that represents today's organizations. We also focus considerably on the rationale for using it, and we deliberately take a business-centric perspective in order to shift the thinking away from the IT-centric views that have shaped the discipline to date.

---

2   TOGAF: http://www.opengroup.org/togaf/, accessed 10 March 2012.
3   http://bawg.omg.org/, accessed 10 March 2012.
4   http://en.wikipedia.org/wiki/Business_Architecture, accessed 10 March 2012.

Business architecture is not just for the global operatives; yes, the larger the organization, the more formal the manifestation of its architecture should be. But the ambitions and ideals of a business architecture should benefit all organizations, be they large or small, for-profit or not-for-profit, emerging or established. We must not lose sight of the fact that architecture is a means to an end, and for business architecture the end is the realization of the business vision. But in reality, we also need to consider the journey as well as the destination.

Inside Business Architecture

Business architecture is a complex topic comprising numerous layers. Developing a business architecture for an organization means taking a 360-degree perspective incorporating each of those layers. We do the same for the business architecture practice, and like an onion, we peel away the different layers of the topic. Figure 1.1 shows our Value Creation Model that defines those layers.

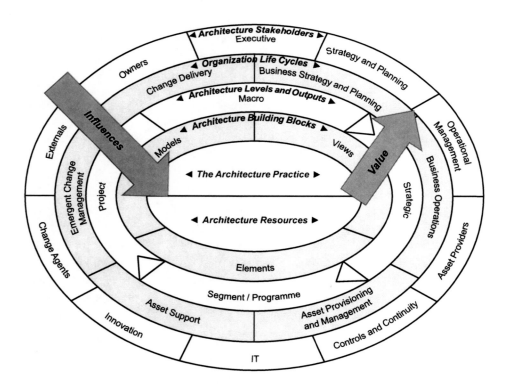

Figure 1.1   Business architecture Value Creation Model (VCM)

Using the VCM, we look at the environment within which the organization and practice operates, and we identify the influences that pose as threats and opportunities. We outline the rationale for getting started, and the value proposition that a business architecture practice can deliver to stakeholders.

Taking this value proposition, we then present the different ways in which the practice can be integrated into the fabric of the organization, identifying ten major stakeholder groups and six major process life cycle groups through which business architects can engage.

Recognizing that one size does not fit all, we discuss the different manifestations of business architecture. We present a Four-level Business Architecture Model, starting with the top, macro-level architecture and working down through to the bottom, project-level architecture. We also discuss the various deviations from this model that we have experienced during our practice in larger organizations. We also discuss the various architecture outputs produced, including, for example, operating models and business architecture descriptions (BADs).

We then identify the business architecture 'building blocks' used to construct the architecture outputs: the elements, views and underlying models that describe an architecture.

Achieving a sustainable value proposition means investing in establishing a robust business architecture practice, so we identify the challenges it faces, its critical success factors, the role of a business architect, and the evolution of the practice.

Finally, we discuss some of the prominent architecture resources: the architecture frameworks, reference models and tools available to business architects to increase their productivity and deliver value more quickly to stakeholders.

The organization must support progressive change with minimal impact to business operations. It must also facilitate business-led reconfiguration to enable the timely exploitation of new business opportunities. To achieve this we believe organizations must be created from an explicit business architecture. Current state architecture expresses a representation of the current organization, whether architected or not. Future state architecture represents the envisioned organization in abstract form that is then created in reality via change initiatives (programmes and projects). The VCM provides a framework to optimise the practice of business architecture and to optimize the transition from the current organization to the desired future organization.

Terminology

Later in the book we talk about engagement principles for the business architect. More than one of those principles highlights the need to establish a common language with which to connect with architecture stakeholders and describe the business architecture consistently. In this spirit, before jumping into the rest of the book we will describe a few concepts and terms to ensure that the meaning and spirit of the text is conveyed in line with that principle.

This book discusses business architecture, but we recognize that the subject matter is as applicable to governmental and non-commercial *organizations* as much as commercial *businesses*, hence we have used the terms interchangeably.

Throughout the book we have used the term *architecture element* to represent any discrete thing that could be used to describe a business within the architecture; we also use the terms *element* and *component* synonymously. We use the terms *agent, building block* and *relationship* to be more specific than 'element': the term *agent* is used to represent parts of the architecture that may be described as active, initiative, non-deterministic, self-minded, chaotic, natural, social or organic (usually reserved for people, organization units and organizational entities); *building blocks* may be described as passive, reactive, deterministic, synthetic, technological; we capture important *relationships* between building blocks and agents: for example, causality, dependency, location, applicability, ownership, command/control, composition, inheritance, or any other meaningful and useful association. Recognizing that building blocks come in different forms and that constructing more sophisticated building blocks is certainly a product of advancing technology, we may qualify building blocks as 'primitive' or 'composite': *primitive building blocks* represent base or atomic parts, and *composite building blocks* represent assemblies of other architectural elements. We generally assume agents to be composite in nature, but we often have no control over that composition.

There is a lot of discussion among business architects of the concept of *capability* and *capability models*. We use the dictionary sense of the term 'capability': an ability that an organization, person or system possesses to do something or achieve certain outcomes. To describe a capability might mean having to create a composite building block, typically describing why it is required, what activity is, or can be, accomplished (perhaps in terms of services), what resources are needed (skills, knowledge, information, technology), what methods (processes and procedures) are used, what controls are required to manage and govern the capability, and what metrics are used to measure performance.

For the sake of brevity, we have used the term *customer offering* to mean either product(s) and/or service(s).

We use the term *organization unit* to represent a real, internal unit within an organizational entity of any size, for example: teams, departments, divisions, subsidiaries and branches. We don't preclude an organization unit being a legal entity within a group of companies. An organization unit is a kind of agent (see previous definition).

We use the term *deliverable* and *artefact* synonymously to represent things that are produced as outputs from the business architecture: for example, business architecture descriptions, reports, analyses and information for publication.

We use the term *asset* to represent any kind of non-consumable or financial resource to which the organization is reliant for its success.

We use *view* and *viewpoint* as described in ISO 42010: a *view* presents a specific set of architectural information to a standard dictated by the template of the *viewpoint*. The viewpoint describes the stakeholder (user), the concern addressed by the view (the content) and other aspects such as format and style. Despite the simplicity, these terms are occasionally considered to be confusing. To clarify: a viewpoint is like a lens or filter that you would use to view the architecture; each different architecture or part of the architecture you observe through the lens will give a different view.

We define some other terms in the Glossary.

> *Success is more a function of consistent common sense than it is of genius.*
>
> *An Wang*

PART I

The Rationale for Business Architecture

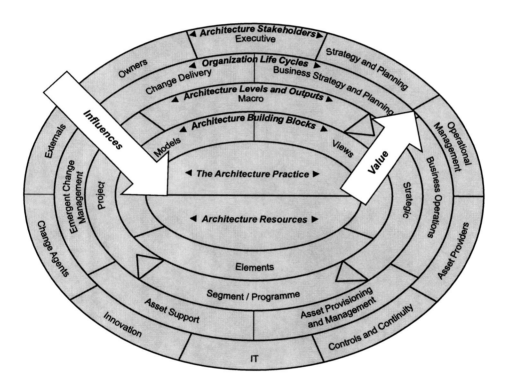

2

Recognizing Today's Business Dynamics

Continuous Change

Waves of change are hitting organizations with increasing frequency and ferocity. Technological and competitive pressure is forcing organizations to achieve greater efficiencies while meeting ever-declining price points. As customers expect more for less, organizations have to deliver better service and greater value for money year on year.

To survive, organizations must provide customers with great customer offerings and at the same time maintain their ability to change or reinvent themselves, and do so with agility. Increased competition fuelled by an expanding and maturing global marketplace and the penetration of technology into the home has led to rising customer expectations. To do better than just survive, organizations must offer something unique; in the industrial age a key differentiator was price, but in the information (or, arguably, knowledge) age there are many dimensions, including, but certainly not limited to, customer experience, personalized customer service, responsiveness, agility and innovation. These are the dynamics that today's organizations face.

But change has always been present, and it has always been a necessity for organizations to master change if they want to excel. Many organizations respond by reorganizing themselves, and others by reinventing themselves. Take, for example, 3M, a company that started out as a niche mining concern and evolved into a multi-billion-dollar solution provider to customers in over 200 countries with over 55,000 product solutions,[1] and Nokia, which started off

---

1 History of 3M Company: http://solutions.3m.com/wps/portal/3M/en_WW/History/3M/Company/At-a-Glance/, accessed 10 March 2012.

as a manufacturer of paper, then went into rubber and electricity generation, then telecommunications.[2]

The most successful companies adapt to embrace and exploit change; others (but not all) survive.

Increasing Competition and Globalization

The response to constant change is not a simple case of modernizing or refreshing an existing product or service line. The Internet as a distribution channel has removed geographical borders and allowed even the smallest companies to compete with the largest. The Internet has shrunk the world and provided access to a global community to ramp up competition. Web 2.0[3] is with us, and Web 3.0[4] takes advantage of semantics to create 'intelligent products and services'.

Addressing these dynamics is leading organizations to restructure and reorganize themselves in a more integrated fashion, not just to the existing business model, but to a reinvented one. At the same time organizations are extending out to third parties and offshore locations, creating an ecosystem of collaborating entities. The pressure to squeeze out inefficiencies of more conventional, siloed organizations is irrepressible. Whether the silos exist as individual legal entities under the umbrella of a holding company or as disparate local and international divisions within a single entity, organizations are focusing on developing capabilities that drive strategic differentiation. Furthermore, they are exporting capabilities from the core to the external reaches of the ecosystem where they are commoditized and/or most efficiently served.

Organizations are eliminating, rationalizing, standardizing and reusing common labour, products, services, processes and technology. And they have to do so against a backdrop of increasing regulation – one of the costs of doing business – and corporate and social responsibility.

---

2   The Story of Nokia: http://www.nokia.com/global/about-nokia/company/about-us/story/the-nokia-story/, accessed 10 March 2012.
3   Web 2.0: http://en.wikipedia.org/wiki/Web_2.0, accessed 10 March 2012.
4   Web 3.0: http://en.wikipedia.org/wiki/Web_3.0#Web_3.0, accessed 10 March 2012.

In some cases, changing the existing organization is too difficult. We saw this with the Internet boom at the start of the twenty-first century. Bricks-and-mortar organizations were just too slow. To compete with new market entrants, start-ups were incubated and grown alongside their bricks-and-mortar parents, and either subsequently integrated or left to operate alone under a differentiated branding. This model is still likely to be necessary going forward. However, the option for organizations to disassemble and reassemble is, in most cases, not feasible because no one really understands how their organization works and which of its activities are decisive in making profit and loss. Rarely can any individual understand all the complexities of today's conglomerates.

The Influence of Technology

Change may be constant, but the pace is not: technology is a major accelerant. So dramatic is technology's influence that it has the power to redefine the business landscape, to shape the structures and behaviour of organizations, to ultimately determine the success of organizations. With such an influence, organizations cannot ignore technology; they must embrace it. As organizations develop technology, exploit technology, sell technology, they must ensure that they refresh and rejuvenate their business models to ensure they are not wrong-footed or even marginalized by competitors. Their business architecture must change in tandem.

New technological advances are creating opportunities for start-up organizations to challenge the fundamental business models of industry sector leaders, sometimes leaving them stranded and struggling to survive and compete. Examples include:

- Amazon versus book stores

- iTunes versus music stores

- Google versus traditional advertising

- iPads versus laptops versus desktops

- smartphones versus mobile phones

- Netflix versus Blockbuster

If those examples don't convince, today there are organizations that can attract more revenue from the advertising on their website than they can from the products and services they channel through the website.

We can be sure that there is more to come; the twenty-first century has been declared the 'century of intellectual property'. If everyone owns a 3D printer in twenty years' time, then distribution of 'print designs' will become the new media content. In the future, will iTunes be selling designs for printing a coffee table, a TV, a violin? Prototype printers are already printing prototype human organs. Advances in body scanning will enable replacement organs to be grown to custom-fit the customer.

The Whole and the Parts

A modern-day motorcar has over ten thousand parts on average, and a Boeing 747 has six million.[5] Each of these has some form of architecture in place. A motorcar has a transmission system, fuel supply system, electrical system, exhaust system, steering system, engine, suspension system, braking system, cooling system, chassis, and so on; an aircraft has a fuselage, cockpit, wings, tail fins, engines, fuel systems, cargo storage, passenger compartments, flight systems, and so on.

Construction of motorcars and aircraft is complex, but their design and manufacturing has been constantly refined over the last hundred years or so. In other words, their architecture is well understood. This architecture is relatively static in nature: once these machines have been designed and manufactured, they are largely expected to operate to the same functional and quality specifications throughout their working life.

The complexity of these manufactured items compared with a living ecosystem is relatively simple: they are tangible, broadly predictable and measurable, and hence manageable. Of course, we do not underestimate the design and engineering feats required to create something like the Boeing 747 – it is without doubt one of the most recognizable icons of the twentieth century. But developing an architecture for something that is constantly changing in purpose, operation and nature, that contains as many dynamic agents as it does static agents, represents another level of challenge, and one that every large organization faces each day.

---

5   http://www.boeing.com/commercial/747family/pf/pf_facts.html, accessed 10 March 2012.

Complexity and richness of capability[6] is increasing. Organizations are using layering, componentization, encapsulation, standardized interfaces and standards to hide and manage complexity. One of the reasons that Apple[7] products are popular is that their underlying technical complexity is hidden from the user by simple, intuitive interfaces. In other words, organizations introduce 'layers' to shield customers from the complexity of their operations and, also so that they can be more flexible or agile. Some organizations achieve this with varying degrees of success, as we have all discovered through using Internet sites and customer call centres.

Managing complexity in this way drives up the number of parts in a 'solution'. Organizing the parts structurally and determining how they behave and interact requires an architecture to ensure that the collective set of parts operates optimally. Also, smarter or multi-purpose, multi-feature parts are more complex than uni-purpose parts. For 'parts' read 'components'; for 'components' read 'resources'; for 'resources' read 'people'. The multi-faceted nature of these parts means that to suit circumstance, they:

- can be configured in different ways;

- can be fit together in different ways;

- can operate in different ways.

With a solution like an aircraft, with thousands of different kinds of parts, without an architecture composed of superstructures, structures, assemblies, sub-assemblies and parts, conception would be difficult and construction and maintenance would be harder. Furthermore, the aircraft has to be designed to cope with the challenges it will face in the skies.

It is not sufficient to optimize each of the parts individually: having each part optimized for its own aims doesn't necessarily mean an optimized whole. A car with a super-powerful engine able to achieve 300 km/h is not much use unless the brakes are up-rated accordingly.

---

6 We define capability as being all the building blocks and agents necessary to provide one or more services, including the business processes, human resources, technology and facilities (buildings, power and so on).

7 Apple, Inc.: http://www.apple.com.

Staying with the car analogy briefly, when asked the question 'What controls the speed of a car?', the answer from the majority of respondents is the gas (or accelerator) pedal. However, other answers are equally valid depending on your perspective: for example, the brakes, the weather conditions, the environment in which the car is being driven (for example, in the vicinity of a school, an urban area), the condition of the car itself and the condition (ability, experience, mental state and so on) of the driver. Like driving a car, organizations need to consider all aspects of the environment in which they operate.

So we see the trends and the actions. But what are the consequences of such change, and what does the new world look like? We are already seeing traditional organizations evolving into organizations constructed from an operating platform of common processes, technologies, information and services that can be orchestrated to deliver differentiated (and in many cases mass-customized) customer propositions through multiple channels. Such organizations are no longer composed of rigid functional structures with well-defined boundaries and interaction channels. Today's global organizations are complex ecosystems that cannot be represented by simple hierarchical charts; they reveal fractal-like complexity when you examine their detail. Business architecture provides the holistic perspective to understand this complexity.

We talk about whole, parts and structures of an organization in this book, and although we make comparisons to complex machines, organizations are not mechanistic, but largely social. Organizations are full of people, so organizations must be designed to maximize the human potential as well as the technology.

In many ways society provides useful parallels to understand the problem facing business owners, managers and architects. Deciding to swing towards or away from employing stronger architecture and more command and control methods across an organization with less freedom for the individual parts is akin to political swings in society: swings between greater or less private sector and public sector contribution to society; swings between powers of the state and powers of the individual. The real challenge for organizations is to get this balance right.

The world is moving so fast these days that the man who says it can't be done is generally interrupted by someone doing it.

Elbert Hubbard

3

Positioning for Change

Business Architecture and the Organization

In an unpredictable world, a competitive business needs as many options as possible to ensure that when change comes it can adjust and respond accordingly. To achieve this it must have a business architecture to create and manage an operating platform that is easily configurable and extendible. Such an architecture must ensure that:

- the internal parts of the organization integrate and operate together efficiently and effectively;

- the parts operate in a robust and resilient manner;

- the parts can be upgraded, extended or replaced;

- the impact of change is unambiguous;

- the associated risks can be understood and managed.

Business architecture aims to define what the ecosystem in which the organization lives should look like and how the elements of which it comprised should be best arranged. This is in contrast to, and complementary to, other change related disciplines such as P3M (Portfolio, Programme and Project Management) which we discuss in detail in Chapter 7.

Business architecture serves to facilitate change and the identification of change *work packages* (programmes or projects) necessary to take the organization from where it is today to where it wants to be in the future, following a defined roadmap. Crucially, this change is not based upon a 'scrap and rework' mentality, but a 'learn–adjust–deploy' evolutionary cycle.

We suggest that a 'scrap and rework' mentality is borne out of short-sightedness. 'learn–adjust–deploy' is born out of foresight: foresight that change is inevitable, and experience that scrap and rework is not economically efficient over time.

This is not to say that disruptive business models or technologies will not force major rethinks periodically. At least when such situations do arise, a business architecture will help organizations to understand how to disassemble and reassemble themselves into other forms if necessary. Relying on Darwinian natural selection to determine the detail of a reorganization in response to a market event may work, but the degree of success is unpredictable. Furthermore, the delay caused while everyone works out the implications in the aftermath can drain the energies and enthusiasm of the staff involved. So the business architecture allows organizations to understand how to accommodate change – whether planned or unplanned. And the more complex an organization, the more the organization needs a business architecture.

As an analogy, we equate the value of a business architecture to the 'ready position' in tennis, as shown in Figure 3.1.

The ready position is fundamental to tennis:

- It gets your body set up to return serve, play groundstrokes and make volleys.

- It allows you to push off to the ball with maximum acceleration in as short a time as possible.

- It also starts the shot off technically – if your ready position is wrong, then you have little chance with the rest of the shot.[1]

Organizations cannot predict the future in the same way that tennis players cannot predict the return balls that will come their way. However, organizations can position themselves to react in an optimum way. They need to respond as well as – and preferably, better than – their competitors; waiting in the wings are new entrants eager to seize the opportunity.

---

1   http://news.bbc.co.uk/sport1/hi/tennis/skills/4230606.stm, accessed 10 March 2012.

Figure 3.1   The 'ready position' in tennis

The Value Proposition

Business architecture is intended to support the management and evolution of organizations. It aims to break down complexity through the application of holistic analysis and design techniques.[2] So business architecture provides a way of decomposing the business in a way that enables it to improve. Improvement may come in one or a number of ways, driven by either income or expenditure; for example:

---

2   This statement is true of any type of architecture: for example, channel architecture, security architecture, compliance architecture, information architecture.

larger customer case

- broader customer case (geographically or demographically)

- broader range of products or services

- higher sales conversions

- lower operating costs

- reduced operating risk

- improved productivity

- greater efficiency

- greater environmental awareness

- improved customer care

- greater agility

- greater flexibility

We often hear organizations say: 'We haven't got time for architecture,' 'It's not adding value to the here and now.' It seems that those organizations don't have time to consider the longer-term consequences, but they do have time to 'deliver'. But they ultimately fall short of success and then try all over again – scrap and rework. There is confusion between motion and action – that is, between doing the right change at the right time and doing the change right, the latter of which is P3M space. Too often organizations are fire-fighting rather than architecting.

Architecture should embody the longer-term perspective, and not preclude shorter-term tactical decision-making; architecture isn't a hindrance if developed at the right level of detail. In fact, it can usefully inform how far off a proposed strategic path a tactical manoeuvre takes an organization and what subsequent alteration will be required to get back on track.

Nevertheless, business architecture is often perceived to slow things down. To return to the car analogy, a car has brakes so that it can be slowed down and stopped. But that also means that the car can be driven faster because it can be slowed down when necessary. So having brakes gives drivers greater control over the speed at which they can travel.

Business architecture encourages the identification and use of the components (or building blocks) of which organizations are composed in the same way that a chemist uses the elements of the periodic table. With the elements identified, chemists are now able to concentrate on combining them to form new compounds – that is chemistry. Without the knowledge of the elements, it is not chemistry that is being practised, but alchemy. We look in more detail at elements versus compounds (as 'primitives' and 'composites') later in the book when we discuss frameworks and methods.

To support the management and evolution of organizations, business architecture must have a viable business model in which its value proposition lies at its core. We summarize the value proposition of business architecture as shown in Figure 3.2.

Figure 3.2   Business architecture value proposition

The delivery of an architecture doesn't bring any direct benefit in its own right. Business architecture is not a solution, it is a tool. In the right hands it becomes an asset of strategic value to the organization.

A Complementary Approach

Business architecture has not evolved because other disciplines such as P3M are lacking, but because we need a way to bring those disciplines together to fulfil a common goal and work within more complex environments. For example, if we look at the difference between business architecture and (business) solution architecture, the former identifies primitive (or abstract) building blocks available for composites and assemblies, and the latter identifies composite building blocks and assemblies for specific circumstances (or instantiations). The former identifies patterns of primitives, and the latter applies those patterns.

In Chapter 7 we look more closely at the various disciplines (or life cycles) within organizations and their relationship to business architecture. But before that, we will take a look at four goals where business architecture has an essential part to play:

1.   planning change;

2.   driving standardization and integration;

3.   optimizing change;

4.   aligning technology.

PLANNING CHANGE

Business architecture can be developed to support different levels and dimensions of change. In descending levels of detail, architecture can be used to inform and govern change portfolios, programmes and projects. The higher levels may describe target capability while the lower levels describe how the architecture will evolve through time using roadmaps. Roadmaps present current and target state views and intermediate views that illustrate the 'stepping stones' or transitions between the current and target states.

Business architecture can also be developed to describe the business at the highest level. If necessary, this can then be decomposed into sub-architectures that in a few cases decompose into further sub-architectures. To illustrate: a global organization may develop a global or group level architecture that is then broken down into regional architectures that is then broken down into country-level architectures.

DRIVING STANDARDIZATION AND INTEGRATION

Driving standardization and integration are classic approaches to achieving economies of scale and scope. Through the use of reference models and patterns, business architecture provides the means to describe what standardization looks like and how integration can be achieved. These reference models contain definitions for the 'gold-standard' building blocks that an organization can use to replicate across its business; patterns can provide pre-defined and tested ways of assembling the blocks. Patterns are particularly valuable when aiming for high levels of standardization consistent with a franchise business. Go to any Starbucks, for example, and you are guaranteed to receive a consistent service and environment to consume your beverage, because they understand how to replicate their business.

Reference models are also valuable to large organizations striving to establish a consistent customer proposition and reduce diversity incurred through natural entropy and business acquisition. There are many global organizations pursuing 'One' strategies with the aim of transforming siloed businesses offering inconsistent products and services into international businesses. There are many organizations driving standardization through the adoption and implementation of a common Enterprise Resource Planning (ERP) system. Business architecture models can illustrate the commonality of business activity and where standardization should occur, but they can also illustrate were local specialization must be accommodated as well.

Standardization also exists at industry level. For example, in the telecommunications industry, eTOM (enhanced Telecom Operations Map) provides 'the industry's common process architecture for both business and functional processes and has been implemented by hundreds of service providers around the world'.

OPTIMIZING CHANGE

Many change programmes and projects fail to meet their objectives and fail to deliver business value. Often this is because:

- the full business context is not understood;

- the business community are not necessarily 'bought in' to execute the change;

- initiatives are led from IT without cognizance of the business priorities, the practicalities of business change, and without alignment or traceability to business goals and objectives;

- the portfolios and programmes fail to achieve cohesion and begin to work against each other.

Having a business architecture underpinning a portfolio of business change helps to deliver optimum results. We believe there is room for the development of business architecture at a programme and at a project level to ensure all stakeholders know why the change is happening and what outcomes are expected.

ALIGNING TECHNOLOGY

With such a heavy influence on business, the alignment and synchronization of technology with the business model represents a major challenge. There should be a symbiotic relationship between the technologists and the management of the business. Business goals and objectives drive the need for technology, and technological advances open up opportunities for new ways of doing business and improving business. There should be a virtuous cycle, so business architecture and technology views should be developed in tandem to ensure opportunities are not lost and threats and risks of misalignment addressed.

Like any other components of the organization, business architecture and technology can be developed separately, but they are related; so their development must be relevant to each other. Many organizations and individuals speak of 'The Business' and 'IT'; we make no such distinction, which is one reason why we refer to the *organization*. Business and technology change and innovation are aligned to the vision of the whole organization.

There is never enough time to do anything properly; there is always time to do it again.

Witnessed by the authors

4

Managing Complexity

The Impact of Size

A single-person entrepreneur can comfortably manage the complexity of their business. They may have a business plan that they carry around in their head. They are solely responsible for execution of the plan. Therefore, their need to communicate that plan is largely confined to other financial stakeholders. They can conceive, plan and execute and improve without reference to others, in a way even small organizations cannot. Their business is relatively simple. The introduction of more resources or 'parts' into an organization immediately increases challenges to direction, management and efficient utilization. Size matters because it drives up complexity.

THE NUMBER OF MOVING PARTS

Organizations are composed of many different kinds of parts, including people, processes and technology – we give a comprehensive view in Chapter 10. If you can excuse the dehumanization for a moment, taking people as an example of a part within an organization: Walmart[1] has over 2 million associates worldwide, IBM[2] has over 400,000 staff and the National Health Service in the UK has around 1.2 million staff.[3] The number of parts in an organization can run into millions. If the objective is to make the organization optimal as a whole, then that requires that the parts be acquired, refined, configured and orchestrated so that they best serve the whole organization, not the individual part. The key challenge for any organization is orchestrating all of these parts to achieve the best outcome.

---

1   http://investors.walmartstores.com/phoenix.zhtml?c=112761&p=irol-irhome, accessed 10 March 2012.
2   http://www.ibm.com/ibm/us/en/?lnk=ftai, accessed 10 March 2012.
3   http://www.ic.nhs.uk/statistics-and-data-collections/workforce/nhs-staff-numbers, accessed 7 April 2012.

This problem extends beyond the preconceived notion of an organization. In a world of globalization and social networking, it is increasingly difficult to view an organization with clear boundaries between itself, its suppliers and customers. Today it is more accurate to think of organizations as living ecosystems that extend outward from a core into the wider environment. Not all the parts are within the natural control of any one organization, yet they have to be motivated to achieve the goals of the ecosystem.

So a key source of the complexity stems from the number of parts and the number of different kinds of parts found within an organization. Large organizations don't necessarily result in complex organizations: a rigid and formulaic franchise business provides a scalable business model. Without planning, putting a high number of moving, different or irregular parts together in a large organization does create complexity, as depicted in Figure 4.1.

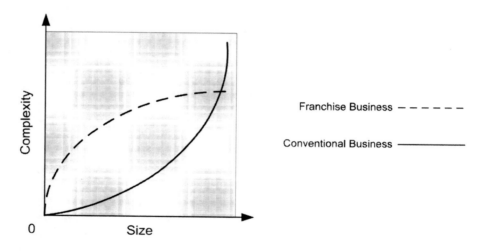

Figure 4.1 **Size–complexity curve**

With planning and strong architecture that compartmentalizes and structures the organization, it is possible to move the complexity line from the conventional line to the franchise line. It is not unreasonable to suggest that a well-managed franchise model is as good as it can get.

CHAINS OF COMMUNICATION

A large organization with a large number of parts will, as a consequence, have more points of inter-connection through which commands and information pass. Each of these points of inter-connection represents a boundary to be negotiated: the more boundaries to be negotiated, the longer the chain of communication and the slower the communication flow, and the higher the likelihood of communication failure. There are many scenarios of communication failure; for example, communications:

- may be partially lost;

- may be misunderstood or misinterpreted;

- may fail to transmit (the transmitter falters or the receiver is unavailable);

- may fail to be received (the receiver falters or is unavailable);

- may be delayed (the transmission gets lost and rerouted, held in a queue or the receiver is slow to recognize the queue);

- may be intercepted and maliciously altered, duplicated or diverted;

- may be duplicated due to poor failure/recovery processes;

- may be corrupted due to poor transportation, acknowledgement and receipt.

When we consider what can go wrong and how many exchanges of information have to occur within a single business day, it is surprising that organizations function normally at all. The list of scenarios is generic, but the consequence of these failures can create very real and adverse effects on a business. In complex environments, catastrophic failures can occur, and the causes of those failures can be difficult to determine, as the list of communication failure scenarios above indicates.

A lack of visibility of the activities in other 'silos' hinders communication and the creation of opportunities to co-ordinate, join forces and prevent duplication.

Variants and Diversity

Unmanaged growth of products and services creates an undesirable trail of variants in process, technology and skills that contribute to organizational complexity and unavoidable overheads. Even in a planned environment, variation is inescapable.

Consider business processes within an organization. There may be a core business process that has been designated the company standard, but there may also be a huge number of legacy and local variants to accompany it. For an established global organization, there could be hundreds or even thousands of these variants, and each variant may require different knowledge, different procedures, different skills and different regulations to comply with.

The growth of product and service variants is fuelled over time by organic and acquisitive growth, continuous innovation and changing regulation. It creates an undesirable proliferation of variants in other areas of the organization as well. Product or service variants drive business process variants. Business process variants drive technology variants: for example, software application variants. They also drive variants in the skill and knowledge of staff that participate in the process and deal with exception processing, and those who manage, develop and support the business software applications.

To solve this problem, organizations spend millions of dollars re-engineering their processes and hitting a wall in terms of return on investment and performance improvement. Frequently what results is a more refined and streamlined process but with minimal performance improvements and support for the same legacy product and service variants. The problem is not straightforward to resolve. Some variants are unavoidable due to local regulation, but putting those to one side, how do you compare variants and determine whether they are the same thing when the likelihood is that they will be known by another name? Figure 4.2 shows that there are at least ten combinations when trying to identify and match variants. The problem is actually worse than starting with a box of puzzle pieces: there are no corners or edges that help to establish an absolute reference point or boundary from which you can work inward. Adopting an industry reference model or processes inherent in the design of an IT system (if they are documented) can help, but they may be far from ideal.

		Different Name	Same Name
Different Scope		1	6
Less Scope		2	7
More Scope		3	8
Same Scope		4	9
Overlapping Scope		5	10

Figure 4.2   Variant identification matrix

If organizations focused on removing legacy product and service variants, the 'variant support' in all the supporting agents would just fall away. It may be cheaper to migrate existing customers from old to new products and pay a one-off compensation fee rather than re-engineer the organization to continue the support of legacy. Some organizations incentivize customers to migrate and eventually penalize those that don't migrate, for example by using tariff structures. When the Oyster Card[®4] was introduced in London in 2003 as a contactless smartcard travel ticket, lower prices were offered to motivate customer uptake. By June 2010 over 34 million Oyster Cards[®] had been issued and more than 80 per cent of journeys in London used them.

Matrix Management

As organizations expand (in breadth or depth), they inevitably experience growing pains. The pain can be witnessed in organizational dynamics that encourage duplication, leading to obvious inefficiencies. Organizations react by reorganizing and restructuring themselves utilizing multiple control structures to achieve economies of scale and scope. Customer-facing activities

---

4   http://en.wikipedia.org/wiki/Oystercard, accessed 10 March 2012.

organize by business line, product line, geography or market segment; internal activities organize by business function. On top of that, each organization unit has to deal with the considerations of different profit-and-loss account owners.

In such organizations, middle managers find themselves working within a matrix with objectives set by multiple managers. These hierarchies have the ability to create parallel command and control systems that compete. Any kind of subsequent reorganization creates a ripple through each of the structures: and it does not just happen at one level – it starts with the large organization units and works its way down through the smaller ones.

The net effect is that in organizations of this nature, every restructuring creates a time lag while each organization unit assesses and adjusts its scope of responsibility and activity. The path to establishing exactly what organization units are responsible for is lengthy, and frequently never documented in a way that avoids confusion and conflict. In some cases, organizations haven't finished addressing the previous changes before the next change comes along. In short, organizations have a tough time keeping up with changing responsibilities and decision rights.[5] Organizations lack a common place in which to specify change, which prevents change from being expressed explicitly (as part of the change's design) or documented retrospectively and consistently (after the change). Such situations have the potential to create periods of ambiguity, internal confusion, conflict and under-performance. Operational managers are sensitive to the impact of change, and especially changes that come from 'outside' their area. They are charged with guarding their operation, and in highly regulated industry sectors it is hardly surprising that change agents receive pushback and delay in response to half-baked or unrealistic ideas.

Many large international organizations have moved away from power structures where the 'country manager' is king to more centralist models where the 'group manager' is king. With any kind of major reorganization, it is likely that numerous, very legitimate questions should be addressed at the macro level as part of the change design process, and before initiating change across the organization. Here are some questions that might be asked:

- Who drives the marketing strategy – the customer groups or the product groups?

---

5   Decision rights are rules that determine the scope of influence of governance bodies, rules for escalation and delegation, and the rules for matrix-managed organizations that direct who can make what decisions.

- Who decides where discretionary spend will apply to improve capability – regional profit-and-loss owners or global function heads?

- Are the objectives set for global functions aligned with the objectives set for profit-and-loss owners, customer groups or product groups?

- Does the group decide what products are sold, where and to whom?

- Does product management drive product design globally or within the country?

- Can regions or countries introduce products variants? If so, what can they vary?

- Are the only permissible product changes those necessary to achieve local regulatory compliance?

- Does product manufacture occur regionally?

- Which product distribution channels are operated at global, regional or country level?

- How is product distribution differentiated across channels, and how are conflicts in merchandising and pricing resolved?

Many problems relating to stalled or delayed transformation initiatives stem from a lack of well-thought out detail that can be socialized and tested prior to implementation.

Negotiating the Boundaries

We have already mentioned how matrix management and multiple organizational structures create boundaries within the business, and how the divisions created can cause problems in communication, command and control. If we now look at an organization operating in a larger country or internationally, a number of other factors could be added into the mix to create more boundaries that need to be negotiated. For example:

- The organization's hierarchies will be broader and deeper, and protocols need to be developed between group, region and country levels.

- The marketplace in which the business operates is broader, thus any hierarchical classification of customer or market segmentation may be broader or deeper.

- The business may need to operate to support multiple languages in its customer base, requiring human resources to be organized by the languages they speak.

- The business may need to operate over multiple time zones, which may squeeze out-of-hours processing and maintenance time. Globally deployed systems have to achieve 24/7 availability, and this can significantly increase the cost of design.

- The business may have to work with different calendars – the Gregorian calendar is not used everywhere in the world.

- The business may have to work with multiple currencies.

- The business may operate over multiple distribution channels, potentially duplicating capabilities.

- The business may operate as multiple legal entities and operate multiple profit-and-loss centres, possibly complying with different accounting, tax reporting and standards.

- The business may be subject to different laws in different countries.

- The business may be subject to different tax jurisdictions – this may even differ state by state or region by region within a country.

- The business may be subject to different regulatory controls depending on the domicile of the customer.

- The business may be subject to different cultures, of its staff and its customers.

- The behaviour of marketplaces and customers can be affected by different business cycles – for example, economic, seasonal, political.

- The business may have outsourced back office operations, creating boundaries of time, language, culture or geography previously absent between front office and back office operations.

Each scenario has the potential to introduce a new dimension of complexity, and with each dimension a new set of permutations that may have to be accommodated across each of the affected functional areas of the business. With so many boundaries, it can be difficult to see the wood for the trees.

To provide a simple example, a bank was incurring huge costs in what it perceived to be an inefficient process because its back office had to re-establish contact with applicants to resolve any queries about their account applications. The transaction cost was too high and the time to complete account opening was stretching to multiple weeks rather than days. Consequently, customer satisfaction was extremely low. Analysis revealed that the branches were incentivized to sell as many products as possible. There was no measure of the completeness of application forms, so the branch staff did not gather sufficient supporting information to enable the account to be opened by the back office. Boundaries prevented communication, and the divisions created by the boundaries possessed different motivations.

A simple, agreed and communicated understanding of the end-to-end process can very easily improve or prevent such situations. There is a need for business architects to operate across these boundaries.

Organizations are More Complex than Machines

To solve the above problems, we cannot design an organization like a machine: we have to recognize that it is more akin to a living ecosystem. Unlike parts in a machine that are passive, reactive and deterministic, we are driven by motivations that extend beyond our working lives. We are agents within the ecosystem capable of being active, self-minded and unpredictable. As we explain below, these human attributes are ignored at our peril; they are the very same attributes that are required to deal with unexpected situations, where the nature of response needs to be fluid.

SELF-DETERMINING AGENTS

As humans, we have self-determination. We each have different belief systems, values and cultures that prevent us from behaving like robots. Also, through different experiences, education, motivations and our personalities we interpret information and situations differently. Unlike equipment or software, our actions are never totally predictable: varying degrees and mixes of intrinsic motivation (feelings, enjoyment and so on) and extrinsic motivation (punishments and rewards) drive our behaviour. The more humans that are involved in a process, the greater the potential for unpredictable results, and even chaos.

NON-DETERMINISTIC RESPONSES

To add to the unpredictability of humanity, the design of an organization must address the unpredictability of the world at large: despite what business process management theory may state, only a fraction of business events can be responded to deterministically.

The laws of physics are well understood – or as much as they need to be – to architect a motorcar or an aircraft. During their conception, models are used to create simulations, and barring perhaps freak weather conditions and terrorist attack, the machines resulting from these models are able to respond to events in a deterministic fashion.

Within a business ecosystem it is possible to find a spectrum of complexity in the causality of events: from chaos – where cause and effect are not understood at all and the factors involved are beyond comprehension – to order – where there is a clear relationship between cause and effect. The Cynefin[6] framework recognizes four key kinds of causality, of which only one can easily be labelled deterministic. Organizations cannot avoid non-deterministic events, so strategies must be factored into the architecture of the business to ensure they can be managed and that the unforeseen events do not induce 'unsafe' failure in the ecosystem.

---

6   C.F. Kurtz and D.J. Snowden, 'The new dynamics of strategy: Sense-making in a complex and complicated world', *IBM Systems Journal*, vol. 42, no. 3 (2003), http://alumni.media.mit.edu/~brooks/storybiz/kurtz.pdf, accessed 10 March 2012.

Given this complex environment, the business architecture must accommodate different kinds of causality, and harness the human potential and provide a cushion against human 'weaknesses'.

How Business Architecture Can Help

Given all of the different challenges that we have discussed, none of them can be understood well enough by employing an analysis or design process with a local focus. Even if they were understood, it is unlikely that a local change project would have the remit to remedy a regional or global systemic problem. Any observation is likely to be very quickly put out of scope.

So the organization is a complex web of inter-connected parts. When we consider that each part can be connected to many other parts, not just in two dimensions but many dimensions, it is not surprising that change is complex. The brain has as similarly complex structure of inter-connected neurons; its shape is non-uniform and it is evolving.

Is business transformation like brain surgery? Sometimes it would seem so, except that many organizations embark on change without really understanding what the organization looks like and what it should look like. This makes diagnosis of problems difficult, and it makes treatment questionable. Doctors do not embark on brain surgery without first building up a picture using magnetic resonance imaging. We suggest that organizations should not embark on change without first establishing a picture of the current and intended business architecture. Without understanding the implications and impact of change, transformation will not be accurately qualified, quantified or targeted. In essence, the wrong prescription can be issued based upon an inadequate diagnosis. Small changes can very quickly balloon to large changes, and of course, change programmes can be expensive, run late and fall short of expectations.

Business architecture:

- Brings 'big picture' thinking into play. This is more than just scope. It is important to understand the business context, and the whole within which the parts under consideration exist – not just the current viewpoints, but also future viewpoints. A broader, impartial and holistic perspective that engages systems thinking techniques can help to address these difficult challenges.

- Provides the 20,000-feet view, the oversight necessary to spot those things that cannot be observed in the trenches, or silos. It can help managers to see over the boundaries and understand how the parts fit together or could fit together; they can then see opportunities for rationalization, standardization, collaboration and change programme optimization.

- Provides a natural home to capture a broad range of information about the business without getting lost in the detail. If the information is captured in a structured form or a model, then it can also be tested prior to implementation; a non-verbose picture of the business can be built very easily within a specialist tool.

Business architecture provides a set of tools, methods and practices for understanding and managing complexity.

> *It doesn't matter how much you want. What really matters is how much you want it. The extent and complexity of the problem does not matter as much as does the willingness to solve it.*
>
> *Ralph Marston*

5

Delivering Value

The Importance of a Demonstrable Value Proposition

Many established business architecture practices constantly face an uphill battle to justify their existence. Architecture practices are often perceived as 'ivory towers' that are disconnected from reality. The architects are considered to be too theoretical and insufficiently pragmatic. It seems that, unlike other disciplines, the requirement to justify their existence comes around far too often for many practising architects. In our experience, this re-examination largely stems from how the architecture practice 'sets out its stall' and how its architects interact with other disciplines and stakeholders.

Few organizations have realized the full promise of architecture, although those who have mastered it have increased their strategic competitiveness,[1] be they public or private, for-profit or not-for-profit. The public sector is generally very open about sharing its successes and failures; the private sector, on the other hand, is, as the name suggests, very private about its experiences.

That said, there are success stories. There are many examples in manufacturing where a business architecture was effectively established but not necessarily recognized formally or explicitly. Nokia as an example, in its rise as a dominant player in the mobile phone market, attributed much of its success to its adoption of a product line engineering discipline. To produce over 40 million phones in a year,[2] it showed that the company could also master the supply chain and manufacturing logistics. This would never have happened without a level of planning and rigour at a business level that we are asserting that business architecture should encompass.

1   J.W. Ross, P. Weill and D.C. Robertson, *Enterprise Architecture as Strategy: Creating a Foundation for Business Execution* (Harvard Business School Press, 2006).
2   Nokia Corporation company history: http://www.fundinguniverse.com/company-histories/Nokia-Corporation-Company-History.html, accessed 10 March 2012.

Focusing on the Benefits

John Zachman[3] suggests that:

> 'Cost-justification' [of architecture] is an idea that came out of the Industrial Age when the value proposition for computers ('systems') was 'better, faster, cheaper.' ... But ... the Industrial Age is over. ... In contrast, Architecture is an asset. You invest in assets in order to enable you to do something you otherwise are unable to do. Assets are reusable, infrastructure.

The causal chain between doing architecture and realizing benefit from architecture is potentially lengthy. Once architecture has been defined, its application in the construction and deployment of a business solution involves numerous individuals and groups. Between the architect and the end user, there is the chance that the architecture is not executed to the letter and so some of the projected benefits may be lost. Conversely, if the architecture is followed to the letter, it may not yield the expected benefits.

Furthermore, considerable time elapses between 'doing' architecture and realizing the benefits of the architected business solution. Often this time span will stretch over one or more financial planning periods. The fundamental point here is that the big benefits in architecture come through long-term investment. The core issue is that business people deal in much shorter-term objectives and financial goals. For architecture to be effective and to survive the commercial pressures, it must make an impact on an ongoing basis, or at least achieve periodic 'quick wins'. Moreover, the relationship with the numerous architecture stakeholders must be cultivated and maintained over time. If nothing else, architects should ensure they have a strong grasp of the big picture, and that is a unique perspective that few can provide. This in itself is demonstrating value.

Besides proving an innate sense of value, architecture also has to promote itself in relative terms. In particular, it must be relative to organizational strategy, P3M and solution design. A common question is: 'Why is an architecture practice needed if the organization has a strategy function and a planning function both setting direction?' Faced with this kind of competition for management mindshare, it is important to establish a rigorous model of how architecture will add value and how it will engage and satisfy its customers.

---

3   J.A. Zachman, *Enterprise Architecture: The Issue of the Century* (Zachman International, 1996).

To this point, you must know who your customers are and how you are going to serve them. To use a commercial perspective, it is a crowded market, and architecture has to deliver something different.

To help to address these problems, we believe that a clear identification of stakeholders and their needs is essential. We also believe that architecture should not be a sideshow at the fair. It should be on the main stage, therefore we believe that a clear understanding of how and when architecture engages with the different 'change-the-business' life cycles is important.

To help with this, in Chapter 6 we will outline a stakeholder model to address interaction at the human level, and in Chapter 7 we will set out a life cycle model to address interaction at the process or service offering level.

Risk and Reward

Why does all this matter? Putting to one side the need to provide superior products and services consistently and reliably, the risks associated with system failure within an organization suggest that, with a robust business architecture, organizations can reduce the growing operational risk.

The larger and more complex the organization is, the greater the potential for failure in terms of frequency and impact. Here we recognize that size may relate to (the list is not definitive):

- the number of locations (outlets);

- the geographical footprint;

- the stakeholder base – customers, suppliers, partners and so on;

- the diversity of products and services;

- the portfolio of assets and liabilities;

- the volume of transactions;

- the value of transactions;

- the longevity of transactions.

To reduce operational risk within the organization, the dependencies between agents have to be established in conformance to design rules to ensure the ecosystem is sustainable, robust and resilient in the face of unforeseen or abnormal conditions as well as normal conditions. Consequently, organizations strive to achieve as much deterministic control, communication and collaboration as possible. The goals of organizations and the means to achieve those goals have to be communicated and ingrained within all the agents of the ecosystem.

Increasingly, more is being asked of businesses, especially to counteract any detrimental effect of failure on society and the environment as well as other businesses (who are now inter-connected too). Looking hard at the architecture of a business is necessary. Failure to comply with legislation or regulation can result in:

- CEOs and directors facing prison sentences for financial irregularities and for failures in health and safety, and fines for regulatory failure and compensation, where reparation can stretch into millions of dollars; BP[4] set up a $20 billion fund to compensate for its deep sea oil rig disaster in the Gulf of Mexico;

- organizations imploding through a lack of controls and operational (and ultimately reputational) risk management.

Organizations are becoming more efficient, but the stakes are rising as they become more integrated. This integrated nature now means that a failure can create a change reaction through the whole organization – and its customer base. Failure previously contained within organizational or product line silos can now rip across every product line and product. Organizations utilizing common capabilities operate with higher risk. This demands greater governance, greater quality control and greater use of architecture.

> *Surely there comes a time when counting the cost and paying the price aren't things to think about any more. All that matters is value – the ultimate value of what one does.*
> *James Hilton*

---

4   *BP Summary Review 2010*: http://www.bp.com/assets/bp_internet/globalbp/globalbp_uk_english/set_branch/STAGING/common_assets/downloads/pdf/BP_Summary_Review_2010.pdf, accessed 10 March 2012.

PART II
Integrating Business Architecture into the Organization

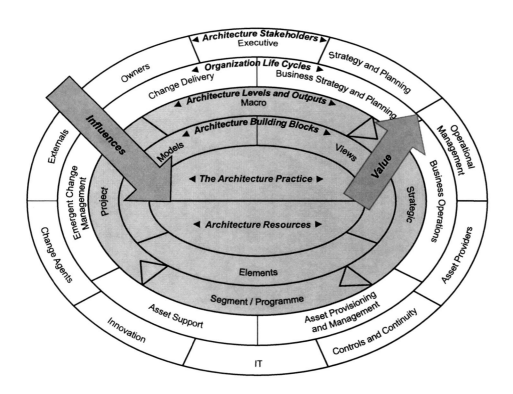

6

Architecture Stakeholders

Stakeholder Groups

For any provider of products or services there is one golden rule: know your customers; know their concerns, their needs and their expectations. The same applies to stakeholders.

In this chapter we identify the stakeholder groups that we believe are key to making a business architecture practice successful. The groups are extensive, but then we have taken into account a broad set of scenarios and a spectrum of maturity of the business architecture practice.

The value proposition of a business architecture practice is multi-sided, as shown in Figure 6.1.

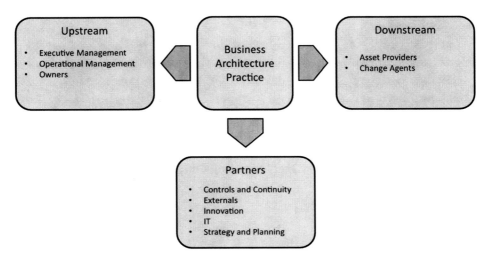

Figure 6.1   Key stakeholder groups

There are stakeholders upstream within the management of the organization on whose behalf the top levels of business architecture are developed. There are stakeholders downstream acting as change agents with whom business architects collaborate to develop the lower levels of the business architecture to enable the implementation of the higher levels. There are partners with which business architects work closely and share overlapping goals.

In the following sections we will look at each of the groups. Within each group we identify more specific roles (or functions, such as the CEO in the executive management group) where it helps to provide some basic rationale for the stakeholder engagement.

At the end of the chapter we have provided a detailed RASCI matrix[1] to illustrate stakeholder interaction from a business architecture perspective. In Chapter 7 we will discuss engagement and integration from a business life cycle perspective.

Upstream Stakeholders

Upstream of the business architecture practice, we consider three stakeholder groups to be important: executive management, owners and operational management.

EXECUTIVE MANAGEMENT

In many ways, the CEO (Chief Executive Officer) is the chief business architect, but as captain of the ship, their many duties are delegated. Accountable to the owners for performance of the organization, it is fundamental that the CEO and their senior executives actively participate in defining the top levels of the business architecture.

Within this group, we single out two further specific roles of CFO (Chief Financial Officer) and COO (Chief Operating Officer):

---

1   RACI (Responsible, Accountable, Consulted, Informed) and RASCI (Responsible, Accountable, Supporting, Consulted, Informed) are alternate names for a technique used to define accountabilities and responsibilities within an organization.

1.   The CFO and their delegates have a significant role in overseeing any discretionary spend necessary to develop the capabilities of the organization.

2.   The COO and their delegates have a significant role in defining future capability for the business.

Why should executive management collaborate with business architects? The answer lies in the earlier chapters of this book. Executive management has been expressing its intent for years, but as organizations have become so complex, the challenge now lies in finding ways to express that intent without experiencing information overload or loss of intent.

What business architecture brings to the table is a means to construct a pyramid of information in increasing levels of detail. That detail can be used to ensure that change programmes and projects have a direct line of sight to the higher-level intent of the organization, not as line items in a Balanced Scorecard[2] (BSC), but as specifications of business capability and future roadmaps. For the executive management, the top, Macro-level business architecture provides a succinct way of expressing the organization's business plan. The (second) Strategic-level business architecture shows how the organization plans to change to achieve its goals, with a rationale and traceability to the higher, Macro-level architecture.

The Macro and Strategic levels of business architecture also provide the basis for important communication (internally and externally) of the organization's drivers, aspirations and plans for transformation.

OWNERS

The major shareholders and investors within this group have similar concerns to those of the executive management, but not being involved with day-to-day operations of the organization, they have a different perspective. While the executive management can use the upper levels of architecture to define and validate its plans, the owners can use those same levels to gain assurance that the plans are credible and sufficient to meet their investment goals. They need to understand that the planning rationale is sound.

---

2   R.S. Kaplan and D.P. Norton, *Balanced Scorecard: Translating Strategy into Action* (Harvard Business School Press, 1996).

OPERATIONAL MANAGEMENT

A business architecture practice does not own the business architecture, it facilitates its construction and acts as custodian, arbiter and governor. Business architecture can only be successful if both the executive and operational management groups own it.

Within the operational management group we have bundled line of business managers who are responsible for major product or service lines or market segments. We also include business function managers who are responsible for major operational capabilities within the business. These include the common heads of function associated with every organization, such as Human Resources, Legal, Facilities, Marketing and so on, as well as any functions specialist to the industry of the organization.

The business architecture depicts a broad picture of the business and its different capabilities. It is therefore essential that the business architects engage the stakeholders in this group to facilitate the design of future capability relevant to their area. The business architects can work with these stakeholders to ensure that each stakeholder's perspective is integrated together, and where potential conflicts arise, to negotiate a resolution adopting the principles and spirit of the whole architecture. As we mentioned earlier, the role of the business architects is to develop an architecture that optimizes the organization as a whole. Therefore, careful interaction with these stakeholders is necessary to ensure that those stakeholders understand that the needs of any one part of the organization must be relative to the needs of the whole organization.

Our view is that Operational Managers are not just responsible for performance in the current financial period but, within their charge as delegates of the Board, they are also duty bound to consider the business capability of the organization in the next financial period and beyond.

Balanced Scorecards can fail organizations if they do not span budget cycles as they are rewarding short-termism. We believe business architecture introduces a time perspective in the form of roadmaps that promotes a longer-term view.

Partners

As partners of the business architecture practice, we consider five stakeholder groups to be important: strategy and planning, controls and continuity, innovation, IT and externals.

STRATEGY AND PLANNING

Within this stakeholder group we include the Strategy function and the business architecture practice. Since the former is focused on developing the direction and courses of action for the organization and the latter is focused on translating those outcomes into implementable capabilities and roadmaps, it makes sense that these two groups collaborate closely.

However, from its roots in IT, many business architecture practices reside within the IT function, and often within a change-related function within IT. Our experiences suggest that the business architecture practice is neither compatible to be grouped with IT nor with the change agents. If it is grouped within IT, business architects fail to gain firsthand exposure to the full breadth of issues facing the organization, and they are inevitably drawn toward an IT-centric perspective. If it is placed with the change agents, the business architects get pulled into short-term perspective of change execution. These perspectives are not invalid; it's just that they are not completely compatible with business architecture. Instead, we believe that the natural home of a business architecture practice is with the Strategy function, as Strategy has the most similar viewpoint and similar time perspectives. In many cases the Head of Strategy may be placed within the executive management stakeholder group as a member of the board, to the advantage of the business architecture practice. As part of that group, the Strategy function can take on the responsibility for the creation of the top, Macro-level architecture, on behalf of the CEO and with full support to the business architecture practice.

We believe that Strategy and business architecture form the basis of a good team. In simple terms, if Strategy develops plans, then business architecture is able to test (or 'desk-check') those plans without actually executing them. This can provide the feedback loop to validate the strategy before it is released across the organization. Furthermore, it also reduces the time lag that often occurs while everyone figures out what the implications of the strategy are as it filters through the organization. Although this does have the effect that strategy development may be elongated, the resulting strategy is likely to be robust and consumable; the initial upfront investment should more than pay for itself. That said, even this 'elongated' process can be reduced through the use of an iterative and parallel strategy/architecture development process.

CONTROLS AND CONTINUITY

Within this group we include managers of compliance and internal audit responsible for ensuring that all necessary controls are in place and working to maintain corporate governance and compliance in accordance with legislation and regulation. We also include managers of (operational) risk, business continuity, quality, security and corporate sustainability.

These stakeholders could easily be placed within the operational management stakeholder group, but we have separated them out because they have non-functional perspectives on the organization. You could say that while operational management has an optimistic, 'glass half-full' perspective, focusing on what can go right, this stakeholder group has a pessimistic, 'glass half-empty' perspective, focusing on what can go wrong. If business architecture is about developing an organization that is robust, resilient and flexible to change, it is important that the business architecture practice engages with the stakeholders who are given a specific remit to ensure these qualities exist at the ground level. It's easy to design something for favourable conditions; the real challenge comes in designing something for adverse, or even hostile, conditions.

As organizations grow in size and employ economies of scale and scope, the inevitable consequence is more parts and/or a greater inter-dependency between those parts, their products and their services. If shared capabilities are not designed to be resilient and robust, organizations will increase their operational risk by introducing new, significant, single points of failure. As motorcar manufacturers like Toyota[3] have found, failure of a common component has the potential to adversely affect multiple product lines on a global scale, whereas previously it might have affected just one local product line.

Having said all of this, we believe active engagement with these stakeholders in the creation of the architecture helps counter some of the criticism this Change and Continuity group receives from other parts of the organization.

---

3   http://en.wikipedia.org/wiki/2009%E2%80%932011_Toyota_vehicle_recalls, accessed 10 March 2012.

By engaging with this group early, its concerns and needs can be converted from being considered as 'red tape' or 'bureaucracy' to positive opportunities or enablers.

INNOVATION

Many organizations are now appointing innovation managers or incorporating an innovation ethos into each line of business or product/service area. Rather than reacting to the future, they wish to define the future. Recognizing the importance of this growing corporate perspective, we have separated out managers and investors in innovation into their own stakeholder group. They play an important role in challenging the status quo of the organization, and thus the business architecture.

Whether they are centralized or distributed, these stakeholders bring an important and different perspective from those within the organization who may be trapped within the corporate culture. Besides possessing a more outward viewpoint of the business, these stakeholders often bring a 'ground-up' viewpoint that is missing from the 'top-down' viewpoint of executive and operational management. To construct a business architecture that is optimum for the organization, business architects have to take account of viewpoints from many directions. Unless business architects engage with these important stakeholders separately, there is always a danger that their voices are lost amongst the naysayers happy with the status quo.

INFORMATION TECHNOLOGY (IT)

Within this group we include the CIO (Chief Information Officer), the CTO (Chief Technology Officer) and the enterprise and IT architects. We have separated this group out because it possesses a unique perspective. Organizations are increasingly bound together using IT as a means to command, control, communicate and collaborate. Furthermore, the increasing pervasiveness of information technology means that even line-of-business technology cannot operate without IT. Consider, for example, the automotive and aeronautical industries that now use millions of lines of software code to drive and manage their product offerings.

Although we could argue that people are equally or more pervasive than IT within an organization, people are at least intelligent and generally more flexible and adaptive. IT presides over the design and delivery of capability that is very complex and very dumb. The level of precision and definition required to create an IT-based system over a people-based system is an order of magnitude higher. Architecture rose to prominence in IT in response to these challenges; because of this, the community responsible for its design represent a major stakeholder group for business architects. As business architects are not usually specialists in technology they need to work closely with the technologists to guarantee the feasibility of business architecture and how it proposes to leverage technology.

EXTERNALS

In many industries that are bound closely by regulation and legislation, organizations have little choice but to work closely with industry and regulatory bodies to ensure they are able to trade 'in compliance'. Within this group we include regulators, legislators and their agents. We also include external organizations selected as strategic partners to whom a close working relationship might involve the sharing of strategic plans.

From a business architecture perspective, collaboration with these stakeholders does not need to be continuous as there are others involved in day-to-day interaction. More than likely, collaboration will occur as and when strategic or long-term issues need to be addressed, and when course corrections need to be made as new challenges arise on the horizon. At the least, these stakeholders may be informed of parts of the business architecture, and at most they may be consulted. Like owners, these stakeholders are also interested to ensure that the right structural decisions are being made within the organization to support compliance or working closely together in partnership.

Downstream Stakeholders

Downstream of the business architecture practice, we consider two stakeholder groups to be important: Change Agents and Asset Providers.

CHANGE AGENTS

Within this group we include all those stakeholders:

-     involved in the management of business change and transformation;

- involved in expanding the lower levels of the business architecture;

- using the business architecture as input to the design of business and technology capability.

This list of stakeholders is lengthy – the full list is shown in the RASCI matrix (see Table 6.1 later in this chapter).

Business architects need to connect with these stakeholders for three key reasons:

1. to help manage the change portfolio;

2. to define the lower levels of the business architecture to describe the new capabilities being delivered by change;

3. in a governing role, to ensure the business change is implemented as per the defined architecture.

ASSET PROVIDERS

Within this group we include any manager as owner of a specific asset or class of asset, or anyone with responsibility for specific phases of the asset's life cycle – for example, capacity planners, designers, builders or operators.

Business capability is reliant on having the right assets with the right capabilities at the right time. As organizations grow and become more inter-dependent, so do the underlying assets that people use. Many organizations are structured with organization units that specifically manage assets and provide them to other parts of the organization. Whether they are fleet vehicles (motorcars, trucks, aeroplanes), facilities and other equipment, IT infrastructure, software or intellectual property, they each deserve to participate in the development of the business architecture. They need to understand where the business is heading and what new capabilities are required. The business architects and owners of the architecture need to understand how assets will evolve to meet the changing business environment.

Stakeholder RASCI Matrix

The RASCI matrix shown in Table 6.1 provides more detail on how these stakeholder groups can participate in the development of the business architecture. We have populated this RASCI matrix based upon the Four-level Business Architecture Model that we describe in Chapter 8, namely: Macro, Strategic, Segment/programme and Project level.

> *Unless you understand others, you can hardly attain your own self-understanding.*
>
> *Miyamoto Musashi*

Table 6.1   Stakeholder RASCI matrix

Section	Group	Role	Architecture Level			
			Macro	Strategic	Segment/Programme	Project
Upstream	Executive Management	CEO	A	C	–	–
Upstream	Executive Management	CFO	C	C	–	–
Upstream	Executive Management	COO	C	C	–	–
Upstream	Executive Management	Other members of the board of directors	C	C	–	–
Upstream	Operational Management	Line-of-business managers	C	C	❖	❖
Upstream	Operational Management	Business function manager	–	C	❖	❖
Upstream	Owners	Owners	C	C	–	–
Upstream	Owners	Investors and major shareholders	C	–	–	–
Partners	Controls and Continuity	Compliance managers	–	C	❖	❖
Partners	Controls and Continuity	Internal auditors	–	C	❖	❖
Partners	Controls and Continuity	Business continuity managers	–	C	❖	❖
Partners	Controls and Continuity	Risk managers	–	C	❖	❖
Partners	Controls and Continuity	Sustainability managers	–	C	❖	❖
Partners	Externals	Regulators	–	–	–	–
Partners	Externals	Legislators	–	–	–	–
Partners	Externals	Strategic partners	–	–	–	C, I
Partners	Innovation	Head of Innovation	C	C	❖	❖
Partners	Innovation	Innovation managers	–	–	❖	❖
Partners	Innovation	Innovation review board members	–	–	❖	❖

	Group	Role	Architecture Level			
			Macro	Strategic	Segment/Programme	Project
Partners	IT	CIO	C	C	❖	❖
		Enterprise and IT architects	I	C	❖	❖
		CTO	I	C	❖	❖
	Strategy and Planning	Head of Strategy	R	A	❖	❖
		Strategists	C	S	❖	-
		Head of Business Architecture	S	R	❖	-
		Enterprise business architect	I	S	C	-
		Programme/segment business architect	I	I	R	C
Downstream	Asset Providers	Asset owners	I	C	❖	❖
		Asset development managers	-	I	❖	❖
		Asset capacity planners	-	I	❖	❖
		Asset service managers	-	I	-	-
		Asset builders	-	I	-	-
	Change Agents	Head of Change	C	C	-	-
		Investment panel members	I	I	-	-
		Change portfolio manager	I	I	-	-
		Programme director and board members	I	I	-	-
		Programme managers	-	-	A, S	-
		Programme solution architects	-	-	C	-
		Business change manager	-	-	C	-

| | | Architecture Level | | | |
	Role	Macro	Strategic	Segment/ Programme	Project
Downstream					
Change Agents	Project director and board members	–	I	I	C
	Project managers	–	I	I	A, S
	Project business architects	I	I	C	R
	Project solution architects	–	I	I	C
	Project business analysts	–	I	I	C, I

Key:
R = Responsible
A = Accountable
S = Supporting
C = Consulted
I = Informed

The stakeholders marked '❖' can all play roles as participants with change programmes and projects.

7

Life Cycles

Life Cycle Groups

If the business architecture practice is to be woven into the fabric of the organization, there are a number of business life cycles that it should plug into. The degree to which this is achieved will vary from one organization to another, depending on the opportunities or challenges being faced at the time. Without this integration, the business architecture practice risks being on the sidelines of change.

Since change drives the need to understand and describe the organization and its business, it is essential to have a clear understanding of the business life cycles that affect, or are affected by, change. By recognizing and understanding how these life cycles work within the organization (who is involved in driving them, what the timing is for each cycle, an so on), a successful engagement with stakeholders is more likely. Understanding the operating difficulties in those life cycles may open up opportunities for 'getting up the beach'.[1]

Rather than looking at the environment from outside the organization as considered through Michael Porter's Five Forces Framework,[2] or other more recent analysis (such as STEER – Socio-cultural, Technological, Economic, Ecological, Regulatory[3]), we look at the internal life cycles and mechanics that respond to the external forces.

The many life cycles at play form a complex web of business interactions. To tackle that complexity, we have adopted a divide and conquer approach: life cycles are presented in groups with a common affinity – with the inevitable trade-offs.

---

1 Geoffrey A. Moore, 'The D-Day Analogy', in *Crossing the Chasm: Marketing and Selling High-tech Products to Mainstream Customers* (HarperCollins, 2002).

2 M.E. Porter, 'How competitive forces shape strategy', *Harvard Business Review* (March/April 1979).

3 http://en.wikipedia.org/wiki/PEST_analysis, accessed 10 March 2012.

These groups and the life cycles within have rarely been documented together or recognized as being inter-linked. Consequently, standards describing methodologies around change management rarely fit together, and in large organizations the change management processes rarely operate in sync like the internals of a clock. Nevertheless, these life cycles do exist, and in one way or another they affect business architecture. What follows is a high-level synthesis of standards such as PRINCE2, MSP, ITIL, PMI/PMBok, TOGAF, Product Development, GERAM and RUP, to name a few. To describe this overview, we have inevitably had to compromise on terminology. Each of these methodologies and standards was developed 'stand-alone' and with a specialist audience in mind. For this reason, our chosen language may occasionally differ in our attempt to provide a joined-up and cohesive view.

We have identified six main groups of life cycles, as shown in Figure 7.1.

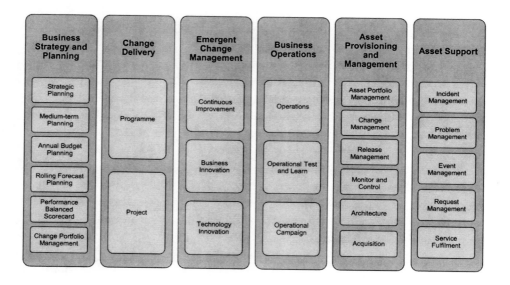

Figure 7.1   Life cycle groups

In the following sections we will take a brief look at each of these life cycle groups. For each group we identify how business architects can interact and the stakeholders that are usually involved. We also give examples of 'services' that business architects might provide. At the end of the chapter we have provided a matrix to show which business architecture services are associated with each of the life cycles.

We recognize that the naming of life cycles can vary from organization to organization, and that naming is often open to personal preference and 'house' standards. We have tried to ensure that the label matches the contents. We have also tried to ensure that the terminology used matches ordinary dictionary definitions of the life cycles and outputs.

To help define the life cycles, we have provided a description and two further attributes: *cycle length* and *forward planning horizon*. Knowing when and how often to engage is as important as how you engage. Understanding the length of these cycles helps to gauge the required effort and the timing of interaction with them. Understanding the forward planning horizon, together with the cycle length, helps gauge the stakeholders' expectations in terms of benefit realization; it also provides insight into their motivations.

Business Strategy and Planning

Business strategy and planning encompasses the typical top-down planning that occurs, with one degree of formality or another, in most medium to large organizations. From our groups of stakeholders, the typical participants include: owners, executives, strategy and planning, externals, and from the Change Agents group, also the Head of Change and the Change Portfolio Manager.

In Table 7.1 we have identified six key life cycles within business strategy planning that we believe an effective business architecture practice should plug into.

Table 7.1   Life cycle groups

Life Cycle	Description	Cycle Length	Forward Horizon
Strategic Planning	Developing long-term vision and strategy	~ 12 months	< 5 years
Medium-term Planning	Setting out of medium-term financial outlooks; identifying business operation and transformation plans	~ 12 months	< 3 years
Annual Budget Planning	Developing annual budgets (discretionary and non-discretionary, capital and operational expenditure)	~ 12 months	Next financial year
Rolling Forecast Planning	Periodically updating financial forecasts and creating a sliding window extending into the next financial period	~ 3 months	< 18 months
Performance Balanced Scorecard	Setting performance objectives for organization units and staff	~ 12 months	Next financial year
Change Portfolio Management	Managing change programmes and projects from candidacy through commissioning to completion	~ Monthly	< 1–3 years

These life cycles are geared around:

- Optimizing the organization's 'run-the-business' operations to maximize its value potential.

- Optimizing the organization's 'change-the-business' activities to ensure the organization is adapting to market conditions and new market opportunities, and that it is capable of achieving its strategic goals.

With respect to strategy and planning, the transformation of ideas into the realization of strategic objectives is not always formal or rigorous. It is often the case that initiatives, programmes and projects are conceived as 'line items' on an investment portfolio, with little substantive information to support the investment amount that accompanies the investment name. Projects may be classified as 'critical', 'essential' or 'nice to have', but rarely does the description of the line item become formalized, validated and elaborated until very close to the time of commencement. The lack of depth in the planning process exposes organizations to avoidable risk.

On the assumption that the business architecture practice has the remit to assist within these life cycles, the principle of earlier engagement is crucial.

Engaging early, to shape the development of ideas while applying due diligence and validation against the business architecture, is the surest way to achieve optimum alignment of change proposals with strategic goals. Furthermore, starting early requires less effort, as the course of action is set in the right direction from the start. Changing the course direction, the executive's expectations and the momentum is far harder after the journey has started. Achieving a course correction while maintaining everyone's reputation is a major diplomatic challenge.

In lieu of engaging with the executive and operational management directly, business architects can start to make a difference by engaging in the *Change Portfolio Management* life cycle. This should be at the practical investment decision-making level, interacting with the panels responsible for overseeing discretionary expenditure and investment. Beyond investment 'categories' and prioritizations assigned to candidate programmes and projects, business architects can help to provide a consistent basis to describe and evaluate these candidates and also enable an early understanding of how different change initiates are likely to interact (collide, duplicate, conflict, proceed in perfect harmony) with each other.

The outputs from this group include: strategies, medium-term outlooks, rolling operating plans, annual operating plans, candidate programmes and projects, and commissioned programmes and projects. Change management portfolios (if they exist as something other than transient spreadsheets traversing email servers) are seldom comprehensive, consistent or cohesive. Rarely does a picture exist of how capabilities will evolve over time as a consequence of programmes and projects. With such fragmentation of information, like a jigsaw puzzle, it is difficult to envisage the complete picture if you only have a few pieces of the puzzle.

Business architects can contribute to the optimization of the change portfolio management by developing a Strategic-level business architecture and maintaining capability models and inter-dependencies matrices between programmes, projects and capabilities (see Figure 7.2). Change proposals (programmes and projects) can be evaluated on a like-for-like basis enabled by business architecture classification systems (for example, capabilities, sales areas, markets, geographies, product lines, service categories, organization units, channels, and so on). Maintaining views of evolving business capability, and how project outputs affect changes in that capability, create cohesion in the change portfolio that would not otherwise exist. The gradual evolution of the organization can be illustrated in roadmaps that show how individually – and, more importantly, collectively – the business capabilities that are planned change over time. Classifying change proposals consistently enables the change management to undertake objective and transparent *comparative analysis*. This in turn allows the organization to cut through the natural but local bias, prejudices and politics to prioritize with impartiality and deliver the best results for the whole organization rather than any one sponsor. We cannot recall how many times we have heard the claim: 'My project is the most important.'

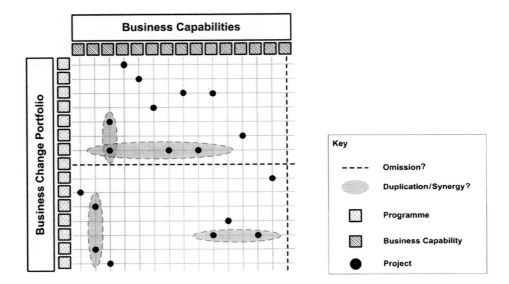

Figure 7.2   Business capability versus change portfolio matrix

Given the nature of the activities and time spent in this group, the weight of outputs should be as light as possible. The aim is to introduce formality and rigour without being overly burdensome. This provides insight that is overlooked in many organizations. The objective of such an approach is better investment decision-making and more accurate and predictable change.

One way business architects can connect is by providing specialist services to plug in to existing business strategy and planning life cycles. Senior management are generally time-starved; providing a 'backroom' service to undertake due diligence (that they would otherwise not have time for) may be welcomed.

For those business architects operating in highly regulated industries, the opportunity to demonstrate how compliance is embodied into the fabric of the organization can be invaluable. It may be that the business architect provides the landscape (in the form of capability models, process models and so on) that shows where necessary controls are applied.

With the outputs from these life cycles, the business architecture practice can:

- communicate the architecture – to inform planning-related activities;

- assess impact – to understand the full scope of change and to evaluate timelines, effort, cost, benefit realization proposals and change programme inter-dependencies, to inform macro critical path analysis;

- carry out a gap analysis – to understand the candidate programmes/project in relation to other programmes/projects;

- provide clarification – to qualify and quantify business problem statements;

- develop/evolve high-level requirements for change proposals – to increase the accuracy of estimating and planning processes;

- identify and articulate options for strategic and tactical plans – to provide the business with different risk–reward profiles.

Change Delivery

Change Delivery focuses on the execution of change to business capability. This includes acquiring/building new or upgraded capability as well as its implementation and deployment into business-as-usual operations. Change Delivery also includes the decommissioning of capability – which often seems so hard to achieve. In a mature organization, the triggering of these life cycles originates from the Change Portfolio Management life cycle, where programmes and projects are commissioned. These life cycles are one-off and temporary, but they interact with the business operations and asset provisioning, and with management life cycles that operate on a continuous basis, operating and evolving assets affected by change.

From our groups of stakeholders, the Change Agents group dominates these life cycles, although almost any other stakeholders could be involved if they are impacted by any one specific change programme or project (see Table 6.1). However, with the growing dependency on IT for information management systems, major business change without an IT implication is becoming a rarity. Change Agents and business architects therefore have to interact with the IT stakeholder group on a regular basis.

In Table 7.2 we have identified two key life cycles within Change Delivery that we believe an effective business architecture practice should plug into.

Table 7.2   Change Delivery life cycles

Life Cycle	Description	Cycle Length	Forward Horizon
Programme	A temporary, flexible, organizational vehicle set up to control a co-ordinated set of projects to delivery specified business outcomes	Programme duration	ROI period
Project	A temporary vehicle set up to deliver a set of outputs, usually in a change-the-business context	Project duration	ROI period

The primary objective of programmes and projects is to deliver business outcomes and outputs. Pivotal to achieving this objective is developing a description of the desired outcomes and outputs so that they can be easily understood by members of the programme and project board who are accountable for the delivery.

It also makes alignment with other change initiatives easier if the same language is spoken and common views/viewpoints are taken across the change portfolio. The description can be used to agree the scope of work and to decompose the scope of work into tangible, deliverable capabilities. This description should provide sufficient insight to enable the construction of a viable work breakdown structure and to guide the detail specification, delivery and deployment that follow. We believe that these descriptions should include a description of the business architecture, given that the business architecture describes future state capability.

Programmes and projects undertake this kind of activity on a day-to-day basis. However, many projects proceed without creating cohesive outputs, or capabilities that are aligned with the strategic objectives of the organization. We believe business architecture should form a part of every programme and project, to ensure that new capability is aligned on a consistent and impartial basis with strategic objectives.

One standard that attempts this is the UK Government's Managing Successful Programmes (MSP)[4] standard. It identifies the definition of a 'blueprint' along with the business case and benefits case as a pivotal activity in defining a programme. This blueprint is by any other name a business architecture description. This Programme-level business architecture is used to define:

- what the future state will look like;

- what the intermediate states will be;

- what the current state is.

It is developed in parallel with the business case and benefit profiles, and is used to determine the projects within the programme that are required to create and deploy the future state.

Although MSP indicates that the blueprint (or business architecture) is essential, it also states that it is the programme manager who is responsible for creating it. We believe that while the programme manager may, in name, be responsible for the blueprint, it is a business architect who should produce it. There can be a tension between the aims of programme managers (and project managers) and architects. Programme/project managers focus on relatively short-term deliveries, and they are often prepared to compromise (which may be incentive-based) on the longer-term strategic objectives to ensure delivery to time and cost. Architects, on the other hand, focus on the medium to longer term, and can be inclined to resist deviation from the higher-level architectures.

Furthermore, programme/project managers are often interim or contracted in to organizations, and their incentives and motivation are geared to the duration of their contract. Quite naturally, those who are judged by delivery

---

4   See *Best Management Practice (BMP) Portfolio*, http://www.cabinetoffice.gov.uk/resource-library/best-management-practice-bmp-portfolio, accessed 10 March 2012.

to cost and timescale are often not motivated (or incentivized) to address the longer-term needs of the organization – they may not even be aware of those needs. Organizations may therefore operate at risk when hiring external resources, hence those organizations need to make sure that strong governance is in place to counter that risk. Business architecture is required as a point of reference to enable consistency and effective governance.

As well as deploying business architects within projects and programmes to help deliver the necessary business architecture descriptions, the business architecture practice should be recognized as the long-term custodian of these descriptions; programmes and projects are only temporary custodians. It is the business architecture practice, as an operational entity, that should maintain the architecture beyond programme and project life cycles.

Early on in the life cycles there it is often necessary to convert a 'fluffy' description into a description from which traceability (from requirements to solution) can be achieved – and this is a responsibility of the business architect. As programmes and projects get into their stride, business architects should be working hand in hand with programme and project managers to mark out the desired outcomes, with responsibility to bring to bear on the larger strategic picture.

A primary activity of business architects is the communication of the organization's business architecture, including its goals, objectives, benefits and so on. That communication should support the activities of programme and project managers. Business architects should work with programme and project managers (and vice versa) to foster a win–win partnership for the benefit of all stakeholders (and not just the programme/project managers and architects).

If appointed on the team in an architecture capacity, business architects can also oversee the requirements management process and activities of the business analysts from a business architecture perspective. If the business architecture practice is not directly involved, then it should at the very least fulfil a governance role to assure that the programme or projects align with the Strategic-level business architecture.

As we stated earlier, too often the scope for business change is set in the minds of sponsors well before any programme or project is commenced. It is important to participate in the life cycles of *Business Strategy and Planning* and

Emergent Change Management to minimize the mid-course direction changes or to avoid failed course corrections and possible programme/project failure.

Emergent Change Management

This group is primarily concerned with managing emergent change to business capability. Change can emerge from many quarters, and often the management of this change is fragmented within an organization. Nevertheless, understanding the life cycles in this group is an important part of a business architect's role.

We single out the stakeholder groups of Operational Management, Asset Providers and, of course, Innovation as key players with whom business architects should interact.

In Table 7.3 we have identified three key life cycles within Emergent Change Management that we believe an effective business architecture practice should plug into.

Table 7.3   Emergent Change Management life cycles

Life Cycle	Description	Cycle Length	Forward Horizon
Continuous Improvement	Management, evaluation, prioritization, filtering, evolution of ideas for eliminating, improving or acquiring new capability	Monthly	Variable
Business Innovation	Monitoring of the business environment internal and external to the business with a view to identifying and exploiting new opportunities	Monthly	1–3 years
Technology Innovation	Monitoring of the technology environment (internal and external to the business) with a view to identifying and exploiting new opportunities	Monthly	1–5 years

What is striking about these life cycles is the commonality of process that can be, but is almost never, commonly applied. The stimulus for Continuous Improvement is mostly internal, bottom-up and targeted at improving current capability. Business and Technology Innovation are most often driven by external stimuli. Within innovation-driven companies, ideas can start from the bottom up but can rapidly be adopted as top-down change directives. Successful ideas result in projects, programmes and campaigns.

Assuming an 'idea' is the core subject of these life cycles, a generic process can be formed. Ideas are registered, evaluated, classified and verified as being new, a replica of a previous idea or a variant of an existing idea. If the evaluation indicates business potential, a fuller investigation or impact assessment is carried out to develop the hypothesis. A data analysis-based approach (which often has a financial focus) or an in-the-field pathfinder approach is then adopted to prove the hypothesis in reality. If the business case remains sound, a change programme or project can be commissioned.

Maintaining a radar of these life cycles is a fundamental activity of business architects. Business architects can play two essential roles in the evolution of an idea:

1.   They can participate in the elaboration of the idea, ensuring its alignment with strategic objectives of the organization and with existing or planned capabilities.

2.   They can undertake an early impact analysis so that the full implication of the idea can be better assessed. It may not be possible to contribute actively initially, so an early course of action would be to participate in an observatory capacity (the 'I' of RASCI) and maintain a watchful eye on what may likely reveal 'lead' indicators of change.

The life cycles listed in Table 7.3 often occur in different parts of the business. Different units within an organization often duplicate each other's efforts – the left hand often not knowing what the right hand is doing. Having oversight of these life cycles enables business architects to add value by identifying where duplication of effort may exist and where synergies can be achieved through joining up efforts.

Business Operations

The group of Business Operations encompasses the core 'means of production' and 'service delivery' now so relevant in the twenty-first century.

In Table 7.4 we have identified three key life cycles within Business Operations that we believe an effective business architecture practice should plug into. You may think that the Product/Service Development life cycle is an omission, but we cover that in Asset Provisioning and Management.

Table 7.4   **Business Operations life cycles**

Life Cycle	Description	Cycle Length	Forward Horizon
Operations	General operation of the business, punctuated by period performance review	Continual	Annual (in line with financial reporting)
Operational Test and Learn	Continuous improvement and evolution of customer interaction and fulfilment to improve business performance	ROI Period	< 6 months
Operational Campaign	Selected and focused activities with clear objectives, and start and finish events	Variable	Variable

This group represents the normal 'business-as-usual' or 'run-the-business' activity of an organization. Once upon a time, production schedules, service delivery schedules, products and services could be planned with reasonable advance notice. Now, in the new expanded and rapid global economy, business-as-usual needs to be flexible and responsive. Organizations need the ability to reconfigure themselves to support temporary campaigns, to create and test product or service variants, to deliver just-in-time customization, and to deal with threats and opportunities without 'retooling' each time. Organizations want to avoid retooling:

- in the traditional sense of manufactural retooling;

- in the sense of changing IT systems that are so important to service-based businesses.

Instead, organizations want the ability to rapidly reconfigure their existing tools and change direction on a dime.

To really understand the dynamics of an organization, business architects have to gain an appreciation of what drives the business from the top and the bottom. There is no substitute for experiencing coalface activity and first-hand feedback from the operational staff on the ground. It also helps to shake off any ivory tower misconceptions.

The primary objective for business architects engaging with operational life cycles is to observe, listen and learn – to understand the challenges faced by the organization. As well as understanding functionally how it works, it is also important to understand the qualities that the business architecture must embody. For example:

- Does the organization need speed or flexibility?

- Must it be ultra-robust?

- How resilient does it need to be?

- Are degraded modes of operation acceptable? And if so, for how long?

- Which qualities are pertinent where and when?

- Which have priority over others?

- When is something suitable to be automated or not?

There are numerous parameters to a business design beyond the functional capabilities. Understanding the 'big-ticket' functional areas is a must, but so is understanding and designing the qualities needed by each business capability. Detailed functional aspects can be addressed by business analysts during business analysis and design.

Engagement with Business Operations also provides an opportunity to gain insight into developing trends in the organization and the wider industry. It is important to remember that the business architect's role is to define an architecture not just for the now, but for the future. Without understanding forward trends, there is a high risk that the qualities required by the organization will fail to materialize within the architecture, leaving it vulnerable to failure at the hands of unforeseen change. Business architects cannot guess the future, but they can observe and, using the information available, help position the business in the best place to respond to change.

To conclude: engagement is specifically to communicate what is going on in the bigger picture and to observe, listen and receive feedback.

Asset Provisioning and Management

Before looking at these life cycles, we will explain the rather abstract title for this group.

We have used the term *asset* to represent any kind of non-consumable or financial resource that is required on an ongoing basis by the organization to fulfil its mission. Under this umbrella we include asset types such as:

- Intellectual property and designs for branding, products and services, people, software and processes, digital media and content.

- Any kind of technology, facilities and equipment.

- Tooling of any sort required to design, build, test and maintain assets.

To many people, this breadth of definition may be considered outside the normal realm of 'assets'. However:

- the acquisition of such things would require money;

- without due care and maintenance, their value would rapidly depreciate;

- with due care, refresh or renewal would be cheaper than scrap and re-acquisition.

Therefore, we treat them as assets worth managing.

We have used the terms *provisioning* and *management* to cover the full spectrum of activities in relation to an asset that includes:

- identification

- conceptualization

- requirements definition

- acquisition; which includes:

      – buy ('off-the-shelf' or bespoke)
      – design and build (in-house)
      – acquire as open source and modify

- implementation

- operation

- decommissioning

Also, within the life cycle of an asset, it may undergo modification, enhancement, refresh and renewal – each of which is a major 'management' consideration.

Minor maintenance and support is subject to the *Asset Support* life cycles dealing with assets in the field. Major change to assets is achieved through a close interaction between the *Change Delivery* life cycles of programmes and projects and the life cycles we list in this group.

So, beyond the Change Agents, business architects need to connect with Asset Owners, Asset Development Managers and Asset Builders. Like the title of this stakeholder group, these roles are abstract in name, but you can substitute 'asset' for one of the asset types listed above to provide a more concrete perspective.

In Table 7.5 we have identified six key life cycles within Asset Provisioning and Management that we believe an effective business architecture practice should plug into.

Table 7.5   Asset Provisioning and Management life cycles

Life Cycle	Description	Cycle Length	Forward Horizon
Asset Portfolio Management	The maintenance of the asset portfolio, the development of asset roadmaps (including asset version and release dates and refresh/ renewal and performance review schedules)	Continuous	3 years or depreciation period
Change Management	The management, evaluation, prioritization, planning and scheduling of RFCs	Monthly	1 year
Release Management	The packaging, testing and release of assets for deployment as asset version upgrades, minor 'release' upgrades and fixes/workarounds	Defined by SLA	Defined by SLA/ asset roadmap
Monitor and Control	The monitoring and review of asset performance and quality. Governance of asset acquisition, design, building and deployment	Defined by SLA	Defined by SLA
Architecture	Holistic planning, design and co-ordination of the asset portfolios and the development and governance of methods, standards and tools for asset design, build and deploy	Variable (3 months– 5 years), depending on life cycle supported	Variable, depending on life cycle
Acquisition	Acquisition, design, build, assembly, integration, configuration and test of assets to form new business solutions	Variable	Defined by SLA/ Asset Roadmap

Although all of these life cycles can proceed independently, business architecture can bring cohesion and better co-ordination, reducing wastage and a loss of time and investment opportunity.

Timescales and roadmaps for Business Strategy and Planning are drawn up for the organization. Expectations are set and dependencies assumed for the creation of new capability that relies on old assets being upgraded and new assets acquired and deployed. These higher-level timelines provide the parameters to stakeholders involved in asset provisioning and management. In other words, they set the tempo or beat within which business change-related activity should be orchestrated.

Individual roadmaps for assets[5] can be developed. However, given the lead times to evaluate, acquire, implement and decommission redundant assets, the task of co-ordinating a potentially enormous set of assets cannot be underestimated. Arguably, timelines are the remit of programme and project schedules, but we would argue that those schedules are relative and owned by

---

5   The asset types, not necessarily the individual asset items.

transient entities. A permanent function or entity needs to co-ordinate and hold this master timeline or planning disjoints may occur.

The critical life cycles for business architects to interact are Asset Portfolio Management, Change Management and Architecture.

This is where business architecture and other specialized architecture (such as IT architecture) are practised. Business architects need to interact with other architects, and in addition to defining architecture, they should govern implementation of the architecture. The life cycles of architecture are really the life cycles of the organization.

We believe that planning of assets within Asset Portfolio Management is more effective when undertaken with a broader context. Business architects can bring that broader context to bear, and bring an independent view when validating asset roadmaps.

All assets undergo some form of change control through some kind of change control board, be it formal or informal. To enable governance, business architects should participate in these forums.

Asset Support

This group of life cycles is concerned with the continuous operational support for any kind of asset in use within the organization. In this context, we are again using our wide definition of 'asset'. In a mature environment, these groups of life cycles would operate under service level agreements (SLAs). We have used the life cycles defined by ITIL[6] (Information Technology Infrastructure Library). However, we believe the principles of ITIL can be applied in the wider context of any business asset – that is, whether the asset is owned, leased or rented by the organization. If the asset represents a critical resource, then operational availability and ongoing maintenance is vital.

The stakeholders within this group that the business architect should engage with include those playing the roles of Service Manager and Capacity Planners.

In Table 7.6 we have identified five key life cycles within Asset Support that we believe an effective business architecture practice should plug into.

---

6   http://www.itil-officialsite.com/, accessed 10 March 2012.

Table 7.6   Asset Support life cycles

Life Cycle	Description	Cycle Length	Forward Horizon
Incident Management	Processing and managing failures, faults or defects reported by users in relation to the asset base (via service desk or technical staff or event management)	Defined by SLA	Length of contracted SLA
Problem Management	Determining the root cause problem that made an incident occur	Defined by SLA	Length of contracted SLA
Event Management	Monitoring failures or abnormal conditions within asset base	Continual	N/A
Request Management	Registering and managing requests to change/ modify deployed assets or requests for more asset deployment or access	Defined by SLA	Length of contracted SLA
Service Fulfilment	Processing and managing requests to change the asset base	Defined by SLA	Length of contracted SLA

Engaging directly with these life cycles helps to understand where problems are arising within the asset base so that trends can be recognized. It is usual that a Service Management regime will preside over these life cycles.

We recommend that business architects interact with the Service Management team and with those involved in long-term capacity management. The feedback gained here provides a useful reminder to business architects that it is their responsibility to develop architectures that are sustainable and which help to create an operational environment that is robust and resilient. Having visibility of the underside of an organization helps business architects to focus on 'rainy day' scenarios as well as 'sunny day' ones.

So, by observing, listening and learning, business architects can validate and enrich the business architecture with an operational support perspective. As a *quid pro quo*, business architects should spend the time communicating the strategic business architecture and the better future that it will create. Maintaining a communication line will certainly help the capacity planners.

To summarize: the principal reason for this engagement is to achieve an appreciation of the operating environment in its normal and abnormal state. Business architects should be designing an organization that is robust and resilience. Without this appreciation, those aims may be difficult to achieve.

Within this group, the business architect, depending on maturity, should be involved in the following activities:

- communicating how the business architecture will realize the vision and strategy

- observing, listening and receiving feedback.

Life Cycles and Business Architecture Services

Table 7.7 shows which business architecture core services are associated with each of the life cycles.

Table 7.7   Business architecture core services by life cycle

Activity Groups	Life Cycles	Business Model Support	Strategy Support	Innovation Support	Architecture Product Development*	Policy Development	Programme Management Support	Business Case Support	Design Co-ordination	Project Management Support	Portfolio Optimization	Business Impact Assessment	Implementation Governance and Dispensation Management
Business Strategy and Planning	Strategic Planning	◆	◆	◆	◆	◆		◆	◆		◆	◆	
	Medium-term Planning	◆	◆	◆	◆	◆		◆	◆		◆	◆	
	Annual Budget Planning	◆	◆	◆	◆	◆	◆	◆					
	Rolling Forecast Planning	◆	◆	◆	◆	◆	◆	◆					
	Performance Balanced Scorecard	◆	◆	◆	◆	◆	◆						
	Change Portfolio Management			◆	◆		◆	◆	◆		◆	◆	◆
Change Delivery	Programme				◆	◆	◆	◆	◆		◆	◆	◆
	Project				◆	◆	◆	◆	◆	◆	◆	◆	◆

Business Architecture Core Services

Activity Groups	Life Cycles	Business Model Support	Strategy Support	Innovation Support	Architecture Product Development*	Policy Development	Programme Management Support	Business Case Support	Design Co-ordination	Project Management Support	Portfolio Optimization	Business Impact Assessment	Implementation Governance and Dispensation Management
Emergent Change Management	Continuous Improvement	◆	◆	◆	◆	◆	◆	◆	◆		◆	◆	
	Business Innovation	◆	◆	◆	◆	◆	◆	◆	◆		◆	◆	
	Technology Innovation	◆	◆	◆	◆	◆	◆	◆	◆		◆	◆	
Business Operations	Operations												
	Operational Test and Learn												
	Operational Campaign												
Asset Provisioning and Management	Asset Portfolio Management		◆	◆	◆	◆	◆	◆	◆		◆	◆	◆
	Change Management		◆	◆	◆	◆		◆	◆		◆	◆	◆
	Release Management												

Activity Groups	Life Cycles	Business Model Support	Strategy Support	Innovation Support	Architecture Product Development*	Policy Development	Programme Management Support	Business Case Support	Design Co-ordination	Project Management Support	Portfolio Optimization	Business Impact Assessment	Implementation Governance and Dispensation Management
Asset Provisioning and Management	Monitor and Control	◆	◆										
	Architecture			◆	◆	◆		◆	◆		◆	◆	◆
	Acquisition			◆	◆	◆		◆	◆		◆	◆	◆
Asset Support	Incident Management												
	Problem Management												
	Event Management												
	Request Management												
	Service Fulfilment												

*   This covers the production and enhancement/revision of the core business architecture products – operating models, business models, blueprints (BADs), capability models, capability roadmaps, replicable business models and service architecture.

In addition to these business architecture core activities, there is a set of supporting activities through which business architects provide support to the various life cycle stakeholders; these supporting activities are listed in Appendix 1.

> *To manage a system effectively, you might focus on the interactions of the parts rather than their behavior taken separately.*
>
> *Russell L. Ackoff*

PART III
Describing Business Architecture

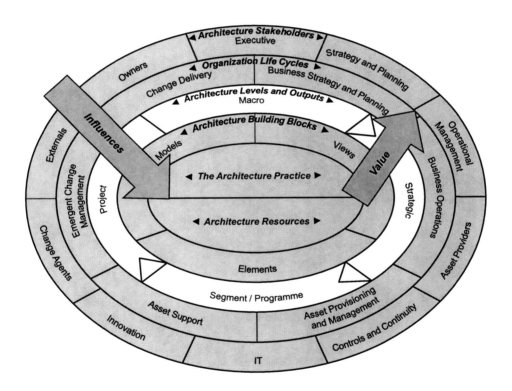

8

Architecture Levels

The Different Levels of Architecture

The complexity of a business, or anything else for that matter, is likely to be reflected in its architecture. Following the human instinct to slice complex things up into manageable pieces, we believe that a business architecture can be defined at four distinct levels, as shown in Figure 8.1. Each level should be discrete and comprehensible on its own, and be consistent with the level above it.[1]

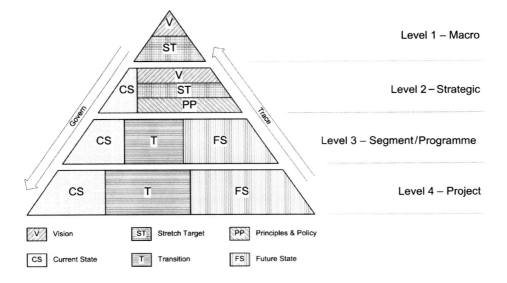

Figure 8.1   Business architecture levels

---

1   One way to promote consistency is for each level (other than the top level) to contain an introduction that summarizes the level above.

Level 1: Macro Level

This is the highest level, the most succinct description of the organization's business architecture. Its target audience is the business owners, investors and executive management. The *Macro-level* business architecture captures:

- the purpose of the business;

- how the business will generate value;

- how the business will *benefit stakeholders*.[2]

The Macro level captures the vision and any stretch targets set for the business. It should describe a picture of the revenue streams and cost factors. It should describe the organization's customers, channels to market, suppliers, value proposition, key activities and resources. Using techniques like the Business Model Canvas (see Chapter 15) it is possible to represent the highest-level view on one piece of paper, and to provide the information necessary to create a compelling 'elevator pitch'.

Level 2: Strategic Level

We have called this the *Strategic* level because its intent is to enable the achievement of long-term, strategic business objectives; it provides the bridge (or translation) between the intent of the organization and the change activities that realize that intent. For that reason, this level expands the concise form of business architecture in the higher Macro level, and defines the key capabilities and solutions that the business needs with, for example, a capability model. Its target audience is the senior management and those accountable for business transformation and change, and anyone else bound by its content.

To provide 'bearings', this level should also provide information about the current state of the business and its environment – for example, SWOT (Strengths, Weaknesses, Opportunities, Threats), PEST (Political, Economic, Social, and Technological) and other analyses. It may also identify agreed courses of action (strategies) to address specific external and internal drivers

---

2   These are the stakeholders who will benefit from the business architecture. These include (but are certainly not limited to): staff, partners, suppliers, customers, investors or society in general.

that influence the organization. To facilitate a consistent implementation of the business architecture, this level also provides the *principles* and *policies* that should be applied during the course of business operations and business transformation and change.

CORPORATE POLICY HANDBOOKS

Most large organizations have corporate policy manuals or handbooks, especially those in highly regulated industries. These state the rules for business operations and corporate governance, and are structured to reflect the different functions of the business. These manuals form an important source of information for building business architecture. Bringing them into the business architecture leads to the opportunity to build detail within the architecture quickly.

The Strategic-level architecture is essential for any business looking to achieve a level of standardization, optimization or integration of its business units. Without this level of architecture to provide reference points, it is difficult to co-ordinate and optimize the change portfolio over the long term. As most organizations have grown organically, via acquisition or without a co-ordinated plan, each part of the organization may well exist at different levels of maturity and compliance relative to the defined target architecture. A capability model, for example, provides a reference point on which to converge. Although this may seem obvious, it is so often missing, hence programmes and projects are unable to chart convergent paths unless an absolute position has been established for them to follow. This applies whether the absolute position is a defined target or a stretch target.

Level 3: Segment/programme Level

At the *Segment/programme* level, business architecture provides a roadmap that demonstrates how the business will transition from its current state to a defined target state. The business architecture scope is concerned with a segment of the organization or a change programme; multiple segment or programme architectures should be governed by the higher, Strategic-level architecture.

Managing Successful Programmes (MSP), when discussing its definition of a 'blueprint', notes that architecture at this level provides the necessary information:

- to maintain the focus of a programme;

- to achieve cohesion of the projects operating under that programme.

The architectural roadmap will describe sequence, dependencies and milestones, but the actual work schedules will be within programme and project plans.

MANAGING SUCCESSFUL PROGRAMMES

MSP provides a pragmatic, iterative process that develops the business case and benefits realization plan in parallel with the business architecture for this level, called the *blueprint*. Its blueprint equates to this level of our Four-level Business Architecture Model.

FEDERAL ENTERPRISE ARCHITECTURE (FEA) OF THE US GOVERNMENT

The FEA recognizes that a business cannot necessarily undergo transformation wholesale, it is necessary to break up the organization into segments. Its segment architecture equates to this level of our Four-level Business Architecture Model.

Level 4: Project Level

We have called this the *Project* level as this level of business architecture is created to support specific business change projects. At this level there will be detailed business architecture deliverables describing current state, future state and transition states to guide the detailed design and delivery of new business capabilities and solutions.

If a project is operating under a programme, this level of architecture will be governed using the Segment/programme-level architecture, or otherwise by the Strategic-level architecture. This Project level is often referred to as the *business solution architecture* because it describes the specific solutions that will be used to realize the defined business capabilities, and it will deal with the mechanics of how the business should work for the area undergoing change. This level of architecture should flow into more detailed business solution design carried out by business analysts.

Variations in the Four-level Business Architecture Model

Having discussed the Four-level Business Architecture Model, there are of course exceptions that are generally evident in larger organizations. The size, complexity and the number of stakeholders makes it necessary to introduce variants to the Four-level Business Architecture Model to support:

1.   international businesses

2.   conglomerates

3.   multi-business businesses

4.   portfolio-managed change

These four scenarios are not mutually exclusive, but each one serves to illustrate a reason for deviating from the Four-level Business Architecture Model. The fundamental issue is that for large, complex businesses, the business architecture, like the business itself, has to be cut up into manageable chunks. Any of the top three levels of the architecture could be sliced into two or more[3] slices to avoid duplication in the architecture: the upper slice contains a single model with common, generalized elements, and the lower slice contains multiple models with specific and unique elements. Figure 8.2 shows scenarios (1) and (4), in which the Strategic and Programme levels respectively have been split.

---

3   Splitting into multiple slices can increase the complexity of the architecture.

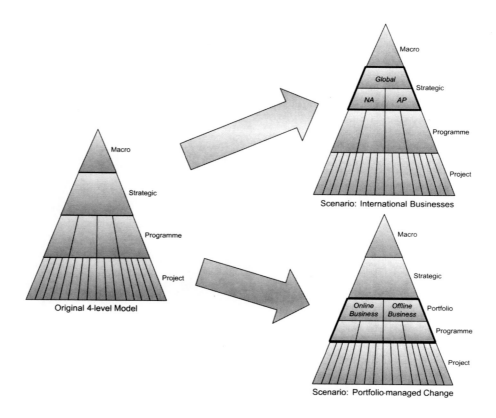

Figure 8.2   Example architecture level variant

We discuss each of the four scenarios briefly below.

INTERNATIONAL BUSINESSES

In this scenario, we refer to businesses that are internationally dispersed but largely pursuing the same globalized value proposition, albeit with local variations to allow for market conditions. For such organizations, it may not be possible to define the architecture using just one *Strategic-level* architecture. It may be necessary to split it: for example, one upper level providing a 'global' strategic architecture, and multiple lower-level models providing strategic architecture for each geographical region, such as North America (NA), Europe and Asia Pacific (AP). It may even be necessary to introduce sub-region levels for clusters of countries, for example Argentina, Brazil, Chile, Paraguay and Uruguay.

CONGLOMERATES

By *conglomerates*, we mean businesses that are composed of potentially quite different business lines and different customer markets. It may be necessary to split the Strategic level: for example, one upper level providing a 'global' strategic architecture, and multiple lower-level strategic architectures, one for each business line or customer market.

MULTI-BUSINESS BUSINESSES

By *multi-business businesses*, we mean businesses that have structured themselves to achieve both economies of scale and/or economies of scope through shared capabilities.

Obvious motivations to create a conglomerate or international business are:

- to generate greater value through exploiting synergies across customer propositions to drive up revenue, and/or;

- to achieve economies of scale and/or economies through the use of shared services to drive down the cost base.

To facilitate this, organizations separate out the common operations and shared services from the customer-centric or proposition-centric activities.

This division results in a business operating multiple, internal, sub-businesses with different dynamics. One relatively common division is 'front end' versus 'back end'. This means that:

- The 'front end', or 'revenue side' of the organization focuses on customer intimacy or product leadership; there may be many revenue sides (for example, in the case of conglomerates).

- The 'back end' or 'cost side' of the organization focuses on shared services (that could be outsourced or offshored) that are driven by the need to achieve operation excellence and lower cost.

Because the objectives of the different sides of the organization may be at variance, it may be necessary to split the Strategic-level architecture: for example, one upper level providing a 'global' strategic architecture, that demonstrates the division and the rationale, and multiple lower-level strategic architectures for the cost side and each of the revenue sides of the business.

THE TENSION OF MULTI-BUSINESS BUSINESSES

It is important to recognize the split between the cost and revenue sides of an organization, and to establish rules of engagement with the stakeholders on both sides so that a strong partnership can be established.

So often there are tensions inside large organizations because the differences of mindset and motivation remain stubbornly implicit and the obligations on either side are unacknowledged. Recognizing these differences and the internal supply chain created by the split can help to harmonize relations. For example, the cost side of the business is always under tremendous pressure to reduce costs and rationalize; naturally, the business wants to increase profitability. The revenue side complains about what it perceives as an under-performing partner.

Many organizations have tried Business Process Management (BPM) and automation, Lean and Six Sigma to optimize the cost side of operations. However, for large organizations with long histories, these efforts regularly hit a brick wall and fail to deliver the promised savings. The legacy business processes and software applications in the cost side are largely a consequence of legacy products and services that remain in use with its customer base from the revenue side. The revenue side of the business must play its part: it must ensure that its customer interactions capture *all* the necessary information for the cost side to process, without cycling back to the customer in the case of exceptions. The revenue side must ensure that it rationalizes its product and services offerings to ensure legacy items do not create unnecessary work for the cost side. The cost side must help the revenue side cost its business appropriately in order that the business as a whole can recognize which products and services are profitable or unprofitable. Harmonizing language in the revenue side harmonizes language in the cost side.

PORTFOLIO-MANAGED CHANGE

For large businesses that have matured to the state where they are performing change portfolio management, it is feasible that more than one portfolio of programmes and projects may exist. In such cases, an additional level of architecture may be required immediately above the Segment/programme-level architectures. This enables the portfolio managers to maintain oversight and governance across programmes and projects within their scope of concern. If only one portfolio exists for the organization, then the Strategic-level architecture should suffice.

Summing Up

We said that these scenarios were not mutually exclusive; the more scenarios that are applicable to a business, the harder it will be to manage the business, and the harder it will be to define and manage the business architecture. Given that many large organizations are managed by matrix, unless there are strong rules defining decision rights and precedence, there is a strong risk of the organization failing to achieve the agility and flexibility it requires. The organization may even work against itself. Large organizations swing with the frequency of economic cycles, from centralist management to federated management, often with the aim of fixing this problem. Unless the rules for managing the matrix are defined, systemic problems inherent within large organizations will never be solved: instead, the pendulum will just swing the other way.

As a final thought, when considering how to split your business architecture, always ensure you have alignment (or architectural views) within your architecture to satisfy the profit and loss owners of the business.

A wise man will make more opportunities than he finds.
Sir Francis Bacon

9

Business Architecture Outputs

Business Architecture by Other Names

Given the challenges and trends that organizations face, it is not surprising that the practice of business architecture is in the ascendency. However, because the discipline is still maturing, its value is not universally recognized. Variations in the approach to business architecture and the deliverables produced from it in this 'pre-standardization' phase of the discipline's life hinder its acceptance as a mainstream discipline. But some of the deliverables that are produced today by organizations that have no formal business architecture practice are, in essence, business architecture deliverables.

In this chapter we will identify some key *alternative* language that we believe falls within the discipline of business architecture. These terms seem to come in and out of vogue, and they are also dependent on the company or consultancy involved. They include (but are certainly not limited to):

- operating models

- business models

- blueprints

- capability models

- replicable business models (RBMs)

We take a brief look at each of these below.

OPERATING MODELS AND TARGET OPERATING MODELS (TOMS)

Operating model is one of the more prevalent terms for a business architecture description. Wikipedia[1] defines 'operating model' as 'the abstract representation of how an organization operates across process, organization, technology domains in order to deliver value defined by the organization in scope'.

An operating model gives a dynamic view of how the organization generates value. It can vary from a model that describes the key capabilities that an organization needs to fulfil its mission and strategic goals to something richer that may also capture the organization's mission and its strategic objectives. Current and target views of the operating model may be produced.

Although many organizations produce their own operating models, often management consulting firms, engaged to scope and initiate a transformation programme, work with organizations to produce them. There is no standard, so operating models vary depending on who is tasked with producing them. Some operating models contain views of the current state as well as a target state, hence they are useful for business transformation initiatives. However, since they are produced to describe the high-level architecture vision, they rarely contain much information about transitioning.

Target operating models represent a variant of *operating model* without any focus on current state. The snappy acronym of TOM gives them a certain currency. As with operating models, there is no general consensus on the contents.

BUSINESS MODELS AND TARGET BUSINESS MODELS (TBMS)

Wikipedia[2] states that 'the term business model is used for a broad range of informal and formal descriptions to represent core aspects of a business, including purpose, offerings, strategies, infrastructure, organizational structures, trading practices, and operational processes and policies'. Hence, it gives a complete picture of an organization from a high-level perspective. The handbook *Business Model Generation*[3] defines a business model as 'the rationale of how an organization creates, delivers, and captures value'.

---

1   http://en.wikipedia.org/wiki/Operating_model , accessed 10 March 2012.
2   http://en.wikipedia.org/wiki/Business_model, accessed 10 March 2012.
3   A. Osterwalder and Y. Pigneur, *Business Model Generation: A Handbook for Visionaries, Game Changers, and Challengers* (Wiley Desktop Editions, 2010).

MIT/Sloan School of Management[4] has observed that there is a wide interpretation of the term 'business model', again pointing to an immaturity in business conception, architecture and design.

Target business models tend to provide a more holistic view of the business; their content aligns to what we describe as the *Macro-level* architecture (see Figure 8.1, 'Business architecture levels'). Whereas an operating model tends to focus on the operating capabilities and often the cost/supply side of the business, TBMs tend to focus on revenue generation and market participation, as well as fulfilment and operations.

Often, the use of *target* to prefix the business model deliverable appears when management wishes to send out a message that a major transition or transformation within the business is sought. Although the omission of 'target' may imply something else, business models rarely focus on anything other than the model the business wants to pursue. They are a must for any business start-up.

We consider operating models, target operating models, business models and target business models to be forms of business architecture. They do not drill down into the specifics of how the business is to be organized; they serve to provide a visionary perspective. As a good business architecture must provide a target for a future state and rationale for that target, we feel they fall fair and square within scope of business architecture.

BLUEPRINTS

Blueprint is a term that has carried over from the construction and engineering industries when architecture or engineering designs were produced as white-on-blue technical drawings.

In the context of business architecture, a blueprint represents a high-level business design. It is a kind of business architecture description used to describe the organization. A blueprint shows how the building blocks and agents found within a business fit and operate together, rather than offering any classification of these elements often depicted in reference models.

---

4   P. Weill et al., *Do Some Business Models Perform Better than Others? A Study of the 1000 Largest US Firms*, MIT Center for Coordination Science Working Paper no. 226 (2005).

Typically, a blueprint is associated with descriptions that show the higher levels of the architecture. In particular, MSP uses the term to describe programme-level architecture. The MSP standard identifies the blueprint as a core deliverable of the methodology. Within MSP, it is 'used to maintain a programme's focus on delivering the required transformation and business change'. It contains information about functions, processes and organizational structure, as well as identifying the technology, information and data required to support business operations. We view the blueprint as being a business architecture description.

CAPABILITY MODELS

Capability models are a form of business architecture description with a focus on business capabilities only. A good capability model will provide quality definitions of each capability, and it will also provide information about the inter-relationships between the capabilities. The term 'capability' is highly debated, and we shall return to it in Chapter 10.

REPLICABLE BUSINESS MODELS

Technology companies often create archetypal business models to illustrate how their technology can be leveraged to enable a business model that may not otherwise be possible. In particular, they produce RBMs to demonstrate how their technology supports particular industries or market sectors. In this way, they provide a more concrete view of how their prospective customers will benefit from their technology. RBMs do provide, in essence, a form of business architecture, and they are often used alongside case studies. The concept of RBM as a business model cookie-cutter could very well be applied to a franchise with the franchisor providing the franchisee with the RBM.

SERVICE ARCHITECTURE

Outsource service providers that take on responsibility for running a portion of another company's business operations may create a *service architecture*. This is a form of business architecture that demonstrates how the service provider will fulfil its contractual obligations. It provides the basis to design the service provider's newly acquired business, to describe the service boundary between the organizations (the roles and responsibilities of each party and the specific services provided), and to demonstrate how it will measure performance specified by the contract.

How Architecture is Represented Over Time

An important aspect of business architecture is the representation of how an organization changes progressively over time. Businesses are familiar with developing product roadmaps: *architecture roadmaps* are really not much different. They are made up of a series of states or 'baselines' depicted along the timeline, as shown in Figure 9.1. It is general practice that a version of the architecture is depicted for every major milestone in a business change roadmap. The choice of whether to build an entire picture or just show the changes is a decision of *effort versus value*.

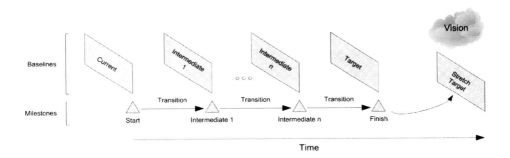

Figure 9.1   Architecture roadmap

- **Current** or 'as is' architecture depicts the starting point.

- **Target** or 'to be' architecture depicts a future point in time that could be described as SMART (Specific, Measurable, Achievable, Realistic and Time-based).

- **Intermediate, Interim** or **Transition** depicts the intermediate steps between current and target states. There may be more than one intermediate state to be represented in the architecture for complex business transformations.

In terms of approach, the usual method is to determine the target state, understand the current state, then the gap between them, and then either work backwards from the target to the current state or vice versa to determine the intermediate states. This is easy to sum up in a few lines, but the effort involved should not be underestimated.

Roadmaps can be produced for single capabilities, multiple capabilities or any other kind of centricity – for example, global, regional, country, business line, shared services sub-businesses and so on – and they may well be depicted against a time graph.

Business Architecture Descriptions

Like many other kinds of business documentation, *business architecture descriptions* take the form of narrative, tables, matrices, diagrams, charts and pictures. However, since business architecture is often formally modelled, narrative gives way to more visual forms of representation. Information is presented through a series of views aimed at addressing one or more concerns of a specific stakeholder.

The key to deciding *which views* and *which formats* is to understand what questions stakeholders need answered. Overwhelming stakeholders with irrelevant detail is likely to alienate them and switch them off. Equally, not presenting them with enough information will leave them cold. It is also important to consider the natural tendencies and circumstances of the stakeholders, and to use their language and their metaphors. Noting that senior management are generally time-starved and the adage 'a picture paints a thousand words', the use of simple visualizations can be invaluable. Alternatively, accountants deal in numbers and lawyers deal in words, in which case numbers and tables or narrative may be a better approach. For the stakeholders who have to transform the architecture into lower-level business design, it is essential to include all information necessary to achieve the desired transformation without loss or misinterpretation. Often business architects find themselves playing the broker in the middle. Consequently, the same information has to be presented differently to parties with different interests. It is a question of experience as to how that balance is achieved, whether in the business architect's head or codified into procedures and guidance.

The level at which the architecture is being described will affect the depth of information required. For example:

- At the Macro level, the value proposition may be presented by name only, albeit an easily understood one.

- At the Strategic level, it may be defined textually in some detail. It may even be exploded out into service categories or even identifiable services the customer can request.

Closer to the Implementation level, those services will themselves be defined in some detail necessary for a business analyst to design the customer interaction and experience as well as the supporting business processes.

Regardless of the level of architecture, there is a difference between detail and precision; there is an art to being precise without being detailed. Being at the thin edge of the wedge, we advocate the application of precision when describing the architecture for the majority of the time, while recognizing that being vague is sometimes useful – particularly during the conception phases of the business architecture. Deciding on the appropriate level of detail will depend on a thorough understanding of your stakeholders.

To answer the question 'What does business architecture look like?', the permutations and options are potentially limitless. The key message is that there will always be a common core set of views that you will use on a regular basis, and you should try to catalogue the viewpoints utilized over time as your practice expands. In Appendix 1, we have provided a template to help you catalogue your viewpoint definitions.

FORMAT OF A BUSINESS ARCHITECTURE DESCRIPTION

Like a report, a prospectus or a business proposal, a business architecture description is usually presented in the form of a document. There are tools available that can present business architecture via an Internet browser, allowing readers to jump from page to page via hyperlinks, but generally the architecture is presented in the form of a word-processed document or presentation.

As with any business document, a BAD is structured and targeted with a specific purpose and audience(s) in mind. Like a business document that contains an executive summary and detailed sections or chapters, a BAD should present summary and detail-level information content. So what is the difference? The main difference is this:

- Business architects try to capture and present the information content in a formulaic fashion (for reasons explained below) –

not just the structure, but the information content, too. To help with this structure, they often use predefined templates or tools.

- For the information content, business architects create different *views* of the business architecture to meet the needs of different consumers, with each kind of view (or *viewpoint*) addressing different questions or concerns about the business. The BAD is just an *assembly* of these different views. Depending on the nature of the business being architected, different viewpoints may be used.

He who has not first laid his foundations may be able with great ability to lay them afterwards, but they will be laid with trouble to the architect and danger to the building.
Niccolò Machiavelli

PART IV
Architecture Building Blocks

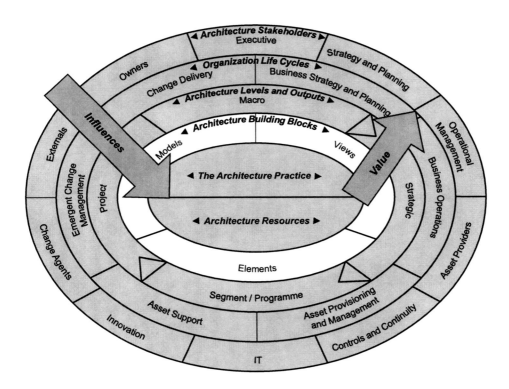

10

The Elements of a Business Architecture

The Business Architecture Classification System

Business architecture represents a clear move away from proprietary business consulting and planning methods that in the past have been characterized as more art than science. In the last ten years we have witnessed the emergence of a formal and open discipline that can truly be acknowledged as a specialized form of design. The evolution of business architecture into a discipline in its own right has been accelerated by its proponents, who aim to move it away from the IT-centric influences that are associated with enterprise architecture.

However, despite progress, there is no common framework to synergize the various concepts, standards and frameworks that exist for business architecture, and those that do exist are not always complementary. Therefore, in this chapter we provide a framework for business architecture that we believe at the very least covers the scope required to consider the architecture of a business.

As a step towards creating a language for business architecture and design, we present the different kinds of element you might use to create an architecture that describes your business. This may look like a laundry list or inventory of information you might capture – and of course, you're right. The intent is to establish a level playing field so that any of these architectural elements can be used individually or in combination.

The architect of a skyscraper doesn't design the detailed workings and fittings, and the same is true of the business architect in terms of a business. In the following sections we describe the fundamental elements necessary for you to describe your business without getting bogged down in heavy detail.

More than just a language for business design, we are establishing the basic constructs you can use to build a *model* of the ecosystem that is your business.

We have deliberately *not* presented the information using a formal, informational modelling notation *vis-à-vis* a data model, as we wish to make this work accessible to all readers. However, it is entirely possible to create such a model, since the core of this information represents a narration of formal models that we have previously used.

We have organized the elements into categories of common affinity, and provided some insight into why and how they may be used to design the future organization. We have left out any extensive semantics for the elements for reasons of brevity, and they already exist in various open standards and formal models. Despite this omission, we strongly advise that you establish semantics and ensure they are well defined, communicated and understood by the stakeholders in your organization. Otherwise, ambiguous definitions will lead to unpredictable results, disappointment, and possibly disillusionment.

We have presented the categories in a linear fashion, almost as a reference guide. The net effect is that each concept is presented quite discretely and independent of any context. The discrete elements form the basis of a '"single version of the truth' about the organization; however, they become more powerful when used in combination.

Organizations have been building information or data warehouses about their business portfolios and activities for many years now. What we envisage in the long term is that organizations will build similar models, databases or data warehouses about themselves. In the same way that organizations run analytics against their business portfolio (to make trading decisions and so forth), in the future they will run analytics to determine how best to reconfigure themselves to address change.

We have organized the information into the following category groups:

- the environment, direction, action and performance;

- the business proposition;

- operating the business;

- the technology employed;

- risks to the business.

For some fun, we have depicted each of the categories from the groups as shown in Figure 10.1 – you can probably guess what it is!

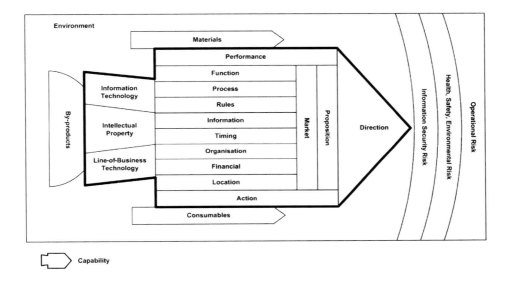

Figure 10.1   The business architecture classification system

Capability

Before we drill down into each of the category groups, we should step back and consider what we have presented here. To describe an ecosystem with hundreds and thousands of different elements, in totality, is a huge task. Even taking a small part of a large organization is not insignificant. In our model we have identified over twenty categories and themes by which an organization can be described, and we are sure that we have not included everything. Within each of those categories there may be three to six major kinds of element we may be interested in. Between those sixty-plus kinds of element there could be numerous kinds of valid relationships that organizations could use to understand how all the elements of an organization are structured together and collaborate together. Even if you pursue a minimalist approach to create a wire frame necessary to reason about and design your organization, it will take some time to build. In the mean time, your organization is waiting, new entrants have appeared, and the economic or political climate has changed. What is required is a higher-level offering that allows you to engage rapidly with your stakeholders. By this we are, of course, talking about *capability*, and it is with capability that business architects start to build the Strategic-level business architecture, and to provide an alternative and complementary approach to modelling. In this context, we are referring to the modelling of business capability.

DEFINITION

There is much debate in architecture communities about what a capability is, and how it relates to *business function* and *business process*.

We define a capability as an explicit representation, or more accurately a 'specification' of 'an ability that an organization, person, or system possesses to do something or achieve certain outcomes'.

CAPABILITY: SPECIFICATION OR REAL THING

One observation we make concerning the term 'capability' is its ambiguous use. The nature of architecture is to capture abstractions or specifications of real things. Though we believe capability to be a real thing, the term is used both to refer to a real thing and also a specification of a real thing.

Unfortunately, the English language does not possess two different words for these two distinct concepts, not in normal day-to-day language at least. So the same word is used in both circumstances – the real thing and the specification of it. This makes explanation of the concept difficult to express, and for readability we have used the term interchangeably as well. We may state that a capability provides services or uses processes, but in reality the only thing that does this is the organization that possesses the capability. This is a subtlety that ties some business architects up in knots.

So capabilities are logical elements of the architecture – 'logical' meaning that they are abstract: they are a design pattern (or 'cookie-cutter') that can be used to define and create physical parts of the organization. For example, within a global organization:

- a *marketing* capability cookie-cutter might be used multiple times, to create a marketing department for each major business line, but;

- a *brand management* cookie-cutter might only be used once, to a create a global brand management team in headquarters.

Confusion often arises about why you might want to model these when you can use business processes. As we state above, they provide a high-level construct that facilitates rapid modelling, and business architects can avoid entangling business management with unnecessary 'how' detail. We don't believe the use of business processes is invalid, in fact we believe end-to-end business processes, usually referred to as *value streams*,[1] provide an excellent way to validate capabilities and ensure they fit together.

A further confusion often arises over the difference between business functions and capabilities. We discuss business functions in more detail below, but for now we can summarize a business function as being a logical description of what a business does. Does this sound like capability? It would do if a *full* definition of a capability didn't include all the composition of categories of elements described in the sections below and highlighted in Figure 10.1. We believe it is impossible to describe a capability without describing its business function. If a capability was described through the six faces of a dice, business function would be one of those faces. In fact, it would be the first face that you would describe. Therefore, when you are identifying capabilities, you are also identifying the prime facet of a capability: its business function.

It is because business function represents the prime facet of a capability that capability and business function look the same from above. After all, it makes sense to name the capability by what it does. It would make no sense to name it based on why it exists or where it should be realized, because this does not convey its intent in the same way. Capability is composite in nature; business function is primitive in nature.

---

1   James Martin, *The Great Transition: Using the Seven Disciplines of Enterprise Engineering to Align People, Technology, and Strategy* (AMACOM, 1995).

If you were to look at a capability from different perspectives, it would reveal its composite nature. A fully defined capability would describe:

- its business function;

- what services it provides to other capabilities (that is, needed to deliver the intended outcomes);

- the processes that enable the services;

- the services it consumes from other capabilities (which is why capability models often depict capabilities in a kind of value network[2]);

- the kinds of skills, competencies and knowledge required by staff;

- the kind of technology and information required;

- what governance and control rules are needed;

- what factors are critical for success.

In fact, describing a capability can include any other kind of element within the business architecture needed to create the ability.

The Environment, Direction, Action and Performance

Within this section we present four categories of agents and building blocks: Environment, Direction, Action and Performance (EDAP). The last category, Performance, we have added because it seems that barring financial data, organizations are poor at measuring performance. To recognize changes in performance, it is important to understand the different types of measures and to use them consistently to establish benchmarks.

Often, the related building blocks end up being assembled with little cohesion. We have observed that strategy is often confused with goals, and goals are often confused with objectives. We have seen strategies with no strong linkage to the challenges to be overcome or the opportunities to be exploited.

---

2   Value Networks: http://valuenetworks.com/, accessed 10 March 2012.

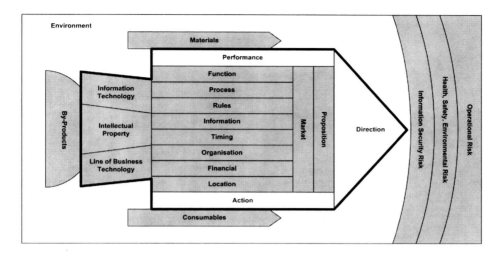

Figure 10.2   Environment, Direction, Action and Performance

Conversely, we have seen blue-sky visions and goals with no realistic means of how to get there. Many organizations possess strategic plans that look incoherent, unfocused and impotent, as opposed to a sharpened spear ready to be propelled at a well-defined target.

The Business Motivation Model[3] (BMM) provides a useful framework for modelling this group.

ENVIRONMENT

Out of the many internal and external influences bearing down on the organization, it is essential to capture those that represent root cause problems or 'lead domino' opportunities. Influences may be trends or events in time. It helps to consider all kinds of influences, including political, economic, social, technological, legislative, regulatory, environmental, cultural and contractual ones.

The BMM separates out the influence from the assessments that the organization makes of those influences to ensure they are understood and analysed objectively. These influences may be real factors, or just risks (this is discussed further in the section 'Risks to the Business' later in this chapter). They

---

3   OMG's Business Motivation Model: http://www.omg.org/spec/BMM/, accessed 10 March 2012.

may be considered strengths or weaknesses of the organization, or external opportunities or threats to the organization. With the foundational diagnosis of the situation accomplished, these influences can be used to create a compelling story and rationale for action that demonstrates causality and traceability to business strategies and tactics, operational principles and policies.

We have identified the following key elements composing this category:

- *Influence*

- *Assessment*

- *Response*

Note, *responses* may be represented by specific courses of action – see the section on 'Action' below.

DIRECTION

The purpose of these building blocks is to capture the 'ends' sought by the organization. The direction in which the organization is heading and the outcomes it is trying to achieve are so often poorly defined. Without clear articulation, the appropriate action cannot be determined, communicated or executed. Poorly defined strategy is often the consequence of failing to understand the challenge to be overcome and/or target to be hit.

Direction may be set for the whole organization, or segments of it. If a multi-level approach is adopted, care should be taken to ensure they combine to demonstrate lower-level targets contributing to higher-level targets. This won't always be necessary or straightforward, since one area of the organization could be acting as a loss leader for the good of other areas.

We have identified the following key elements composing this category:

- *Vision;*

- *Goals* (expanding the vision);

- *Objectives* (that are SMART and expand the goals and are likely candidates for inclusion within a BSC).

ACTION

The purpose of these building blocks is to define the means to achieve the ends sought by the organization with reference to the direction building blocks, and to address factors influencing the organization, with reference to the environment building blocks.

We have identified the following key elements composing this category:

- *Mission* states the day-to-day purpose of the organization.

- *Strategies* define the long-term, continuous courses of action to be taken to achieve goals.

- *Tactics* (that are SMART and contribute to the strategies) address objectives. Tactics may include the following as vehicles through which clear action can be managed and executed:
  - programmes
  - projects
  - initiatives
  - campaigns

PERFORMANCE

The purpose of this category is not to capture the organization's performance, but to establish repeatable means by which the organization can measure its performance. Establishing a classification containing types of measurement and types of benefit will enable a consistent approach to measurement across the business. The ability to measure, diagnose and respond to results is a sure indication of an organization's maturity and sustainability, but to achieve this, a level playing field must be created to ensure a common interpretation of the data.

Measurement represents one of the fundamental capabilities underpinning the Plan–Do–Check–Act cycle advocated by Deming[4] and Six Sigma[5] created by Motorola. The US Federal Government's FEA provides an example of a Performance Reference Model (PRM) – see Chapter 15. As part of defining

---

4   http://en.wikipedia.org/wiki/PDCA, accessed 10 March 2012.
5   http://en.wikipedia.org/wiki/Six_Sigma, accessed 10 March 2012.

these building blocks, they can be mapped against the four quadrants of the BSC and then used in conjunction with the direction building blocks.

We have identified the following key elements composing this category:

- *Measurement Categories* and *Measurement Types* to address operational performance;

- *Benefit Categories* and *Benefit Types* to address effectiveness of business change.

COMBINING THIS INFORMATION

To finish on this group of categories, there is no substitute for thoroughly understanding your organization's situation and the root cause problems that create the hurdles it has to jump. We are advocating no method here other than at the very least to capture this information consistently, simply, and in a way that it can be used to create traceability and demonstrate causality and rationale for the other parts of the business architecture. Be clear about your environmental influences, what they mean to the organization, what your ends are and which means you plan to use to meet each end.

Table 10.1 shows how these elements can be combined for validation and to build a cohesive business architecture.

To give a further illustration, Figure 10.3 shows how insight can be gained from analysing the contribution that each project and programme of a business change portfolio makes to each corporate goal. Using this simple view, we can understand which programmes and projects are addressing each corporate goal and whether there are any corporate goals not served by a change programme or project. Conversely, we can understand whether we have any programmes or projects that are not aligned to any specific corporate goal. We can observe potential duplication across programmes and/or potential opportunities reorganizing projects under different programmes.

Table 10.1 Matrix viewpoints of EDAP

	Vision	Goal	Objective	Measurement Type	Mission	Strategy	Tactic	Benefit Type	Influence	Assessment
Vision		◆			◆				◆	
Goal			◆	◆	◆	❖			❖	
Objective				◆			◆		◆	
Mission						◆			◆	
Strategy							◆	◆	❖	
Tactic								◆	◆	
Influence									◆	◆

◆   Mark useful combinations for matrices.

❖   Mark useful combinations used in example below.

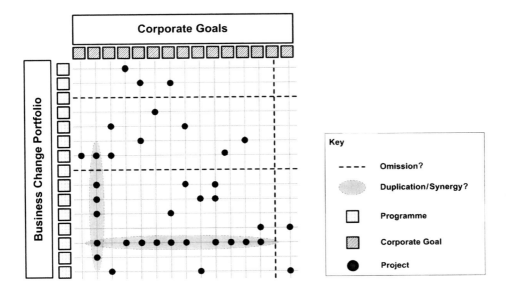

Figure 10.3   Corporate goal versus change portfolio matrix

To illustrate further, we can show (in the text below and using the intersections marked ❖ in Table 10.1) how with one strategy, one goal and one influence, combined with three relationships, it is possible to develop a cohesive, albeit simple, story and rationale:

- Exerting tighter control of travel expenses (as a strategy) will achieve a reduction in travel expenses (as a goal).

- Exerting tighter control of travel expenses (as a strategy) is a response to economic downturn (as an influence).

- Economic downturn (as an influence) will necessitate a reduction in travel expenses (as a goal).

The inclusion of specific measures would result in an *objective* – for example, a reduction in travel expenses by 10 per cent in the next year.

The model can be expanded further into a more sophisticated systems thinking model, as some goals may be intermediate and lead to other goals. Also, events and trends forming the influences string together into casual chains. To illustrate: economic downturn influences customer purchasing which influences sales income which influences profit. Similarly, a reduction in travel expenses is just an intermediate goal contributing towards protecting profit ratio. Such models can be used to codify the logic and rationale as an output of the planning process.

This may seem simplistic but it is worth recognizing that, in the heat of battle, we are all capable of losing sight of the fundamentals of the business. Business architecture provides a medium to describe the fundamentals of the business.

The Business Proposition

In this group of categories we focus on the proposition to the customer and how the organization reaches the marketplace and the customer. These building blocks are the focus of the revenue side of the business.

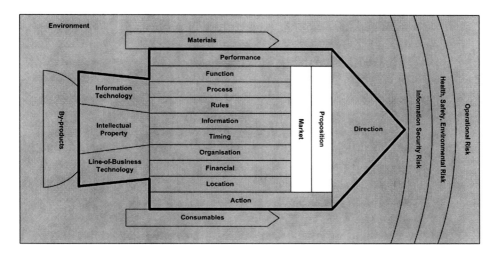

Figure 10.4   The business proposition

PROPOSITION

We have identified the following key elements composing this category:

- *Business Concept*

- *Value Proposition*

- *Service Categories* and *Services*

- *Product Categories* and *Products*

The *Business Concept* should state key dynamics of the business model: whether it is driven by product innovation, customer intimacy or operational excellence; whether its business is driven by high-volume/commodity or low-volume/customized offerings; whether the model relies on creating a network of inter-dependent customers.

The *Value Proposition* needs, as a minimum, to state the primary benefit to the primary customer segment and describe how the organization creates value. Is the customer offering services or products? The handbook *Business Model Generation*, for example, notes 11 kinds of value creation, as follows:

1.   *Newness* – for example, a new product/service.

2.   *Performance* – for example, a product/service improvement.

3.   *Customization* – for example, personalizing a product/service.

4.   *'Getting the job done'* – for example, use of outsourced services.

5.   *Design* – for example, product aesthetics.

6.   *Brand/status* – for example, lifestyle.

7.   *Price* – for example, product/service price competitiveness.

8.   *Cost reduction* – for example, product rental in place of purchase.

9.   *Risk reduction* – for example, product warranties.

10. *Accessibility* – for example, 'pay as you go' products.

11. *Convenience/usability* – for example, 'on demand' media.

Expanding on the value proposition, this category should capture the key service categories and services and/or product categories and products that form the customer offering. What seems like an apparently obvious classification of what the business offers often seems so elusive.

MARKET

This category could be called 'Go to Market', for the intent is to describe the means by which the organization reaches its target market and to define what customer segments the organization is aiming to reach.

The two primary elements we have identified here are:

- *Customer Segment*, and

- *Channel*.

Like most of the building blocks within the business architecture, *Customer Segment* is by its nature an abstract archetype. It is used to represent the profile of a group of self-referencing customers with a common affinity. Understanding the size of these segments is essential, not just for financial planning, but also for designing business capability that can support the proposed demand. The *Channel* represents the means by which services or products are delivered to the customer. The nature of these channels can vary: physical or electronic; in person or remote; push or pull; direct or indirect. Understanding the specific nature and use of each channel is necessary to ensure that each has the qualities and capacity to support intended patterns and volumes of trade.

We haven't mentioned 'market' in the context of where trade is carried out as this is described in the 'Location' section below.

COMBINING THIS INFORMATION

We have looked at the building blocks individually by category, but there is more value in understanding how these building blocks combine. By building simple matrices, we can understand at a glance what products are being sold to whom and through what channel. We have added influences due to their uncontrollable tendency to throw a business off course.

Table 10.2   Matrix viewpoints of Business Proposition

	Channel	Customer Offering	Market	Customer Segment	Measurement Type	Influence
Channel		◆	◆	◆	◆	◆
Customer Offering			◆	◆	◆	◆
Market				◆	◆	◆
Customer Segment					◆	◆
Influence						◆

As Table 10.2 illustrates, these elements all inter-relate.

Operating the Business

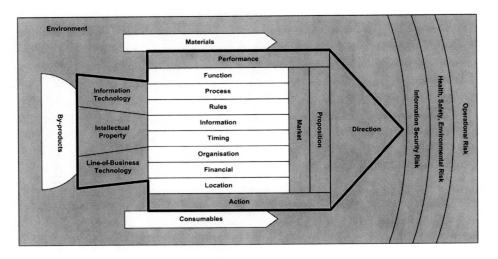

Figure 10.5   Operating the business

This group of categories presents elements concerned with the operation or 'means of production'. More specifically, we have decomposed the area into the following categories:

- *Functions*

- *Processes*

- *Rules*

- *Information*

- *Timing*

- *Organization*

- *Financial*

- *Location*

- *Materials, Consumables* and *By-products*

FUNCTIONS

The *Function* elements describe what the organization does. We have identified the following key elements composing this category:

- *Business Function Group*, which aggregates;

- *Business Functions*, which decompose into;

- *Business Sub-functions*.

Services describe more specific information about what a *Business Function* or *Business Sub-function* does.

Business functions are not units within an organization; they are logical sets of business activity, each with their own distinct purpose. Business functions are generally based on affinities associated with human rather than non-human attributes (for example, knowledge, language, culture, values, skills and competencies) that produce common types of output. An organization unit can undertake more than one business function. The marketing department may undertake the marketing business function, but it may also undertake brand management and public relations management functions. The sharing of business functions under one organization unit occurs because of the affinity mentioned above.

It seems that the distinction between the logical business functions and the physical organization units is not always appreciated. When business functions are not functioning, they often just get moved from one physical organization unit to another.

The relationship between functions and processes is often debated, but their *close* relationship is clear: *business functions* focus on the 'what', while *business processes* focus on the 'how'. At a more detailed level, *services* that describe *functions* in more detail are enacted by *business processes*. These *business processes* have inputs and outputs, and respond to, and generate, events, and they have a start and a finish. They can be triggered when a *service* is requested. Ownership of process is more often than not assigned to business function heads, or rather the heads of the organization assigned the business function. The ownership of value streams (business process chains) that cut across multiple business functions required to drive cross-organizational efficiency is often missing. We cannot recommend highly enough establishing this level of ownership.

PROCESSES

The *Process* elements represent the core means to describe how the organization 'does business'. We have identified the following key elements composing this category:

- *Value Chain*

- *Value Stream*

- *Process*

- *Sub-process*

- *Tasks*

- *Procedures*

- *Business Event*

These are common to most business process management standards, although there are multiple standards with variations in notation and the semantics that do not always match up. Our experience is that you will have to adopt and modify some of the semantics to meet the needs of your organization.

The use of these process constructs is applicable where the organization is able to respond to the business event deterministically, or put another way, in a pre-defined way. Over and above this, there are methods or practices that are composed of *process patterns* that represent packages of reusable *tasks* defined in methodologies and used within projects to build up the work breakdown structures in project schedules.

The level at which the business architecture is being developed will determine the level at which processes are defined. At the Strategic level, value streams should be used to demonstrate the critical end-to-end chain of businesses that are necessary to support the business model. At the lower levels, *processes* and the constituent sub-processes will define how the organization will respond to key business events. Defining the *sub-processes* will necessarily require identification of *tasks*, often represented in 'swimlane' diagrams. *Procedures* define the process implementation.

Business process definitions can be linked to other building blocks to create process-centric views demonstrating, for example, the suppliers and customers of the process and the inputs and outputs. Linked with internal roles and business functions, the architecture can demonstrate who performs what process. Business processes can also be linked with technology – for example, business applications to connect the business architecture with more specialist technology architectures.

We have presented a pragmatic and synergized set of constructs in response to the competing standards and bodies of knowledge that include Michael Porter, James Martin, BPMN (Business Process Model and Notation), UML (Unified Modelling Language), EPC (Event-driven Process Chain), IDEF (Integration Definition), SPEM (Software and systems Process Engineering Metamodel specification), LEAN and Six Sigma. One of the challenges for business architects in this area is putting the stakes in the ground and building consensus around agreed concepts, with the inevitable compromises and trade-offs.

RULES

Within a business there are likely to be many kinds of business rules. Some may be mandatory, and some may be advisory. Some may be designed to capture logic to enable automation within software systems, and some for humans to interpret and follow. For the purposes of business architecture, we shall concentrate on the latter.

Organizations are required to adhere – and prove adherence – to regulations and legislation for their processes and customer offerings. Despite the penalties for non-compliance, ranging from financial penalty to loss of operating licences to jail sentences, it is frequently the case that demonstrating linkage down into process and customer offerings is a major challenge. This is unintentional; it is the complexity of the number and combination of components that makes the linking so difficult. We believe that developing a lightweight, holistic business architecture model can help to solve this problem. Furthermore, such a model can be used to capture the local variations that are critical to understand before a standardization programme begins in earnest.

We have identified the following key elements composing this category:

- *Principles* provide the highest-level guidance that act as 'bearing points' for the organization.

- *Policies* enable adherence of the principles and lay down the rules for internal controls and compliance to external regulation and legislation.

- *Directives* – as the intricacies of developing policy can become bogged down and mixed up within implementation, we recommend splitting out the implementation. The policy becomes cleaner and easier to develop. It also remains more static and reusable. The statements of policy implementation – for which they can be many in a large organization, for example by legal entity – can be codified into succinct statements of directive.

- As stated above, formal recognition of *legislation, regulation* and *taxation* enables the building of traceability into other areas of the business architecture beyond policy, particularly down into processes and customer offerings.

- Finally, the rules that we have referred to as *decision rights.* These are rules that determine the scope of influence of governance bodies, rules for escalation and delegation, and the rules for matrix-managed organizations that direct who can make what decisions.

INFORMATION

Experience reinforces the military strategy theory that wars are won through access to superior information. Having the right information, and information infrastructure, enables strategy; having high-quality information enables effective and successful tactics. Regardless of the strengths or weaknesses of an organization's position, the right course of action can be taken if high-quality information is available to inform its circumstances and decision-making.

In a competitive environment away from the battlefield – whether commercial, political, social or technological – the same applies.

We recommend considering the informational aspects of business architecture at two levels:

- the *operations* level;

- the *semantic* level.

The latter enables the former.

MODELLING THE ORGANIZATION'S INFORMATION

Setting out a simple model of, say, the 15–20 key information entities (and the relationships between them) on a page of A4, with concise, specific descriptions can be a potent way to promote a common language across the organization.

Operations

The intent of this category of elements is not to describe the minutiae, but to ensure that the infrastructure is appropriate to support the environment and operation of the business.

Understanding what kind of information is required for the success of your business is as critical as understanding its qualities. If you have the information you want but it is of poor quality, it is as good as useless and as bad as dangerous. For the key information, you need to know how up-to-date it is, how quickly you need it, when you need it, how accurate it is and how reliable it is. You may need to specify who can and cannot have access to the information if it is sensitive, and what the rules are for gaining access to it. You may wish to know whether it is known only by you, and how long it will be before your competitors possess it. If you think information currency is not significant, think again. By way of example, Wall Street banks are moving their data centres 1 kilometre north to Hudson Street so they can be 8 millionths of a second closer to the access points of the physical Internet backbone.[6]

Semantics

The *linear* growth of staff within an organization *exponentially* increases the challenges of communication. The ability to communicate the intents and directions of the organization, to issue command and exert control, to understand the environment and to create the future demands a common language. Common language is required to span the different operational areas, to enable design of the business, and to span and unify a workforce with different cultures, spoken languages, education, values, knowledge and skills. However, 'high-level' ideas and concepts can mask the truth of ambiguity and confusion. It generally takes the collapse of change programmes and business initiatives for the emperor's clothes to be openly observed by all. Conflict, misunderstanding, talking at cross-purposes – all these represent symptoms of poor communication and the absence of common language.

IF YOUR BUSINESS GOALS ARE TO SIMPLIFY, STANDARDIZE AND INTEGRATE YOUR BUSINESS, START HERE

1. **Define** your common language and your common concepts.

2. **Share** and promote the language across your organization. Only when a common model is understood can the process of convergence gain an unstoppable momentum.

3. **Manage** and **evolve** its growth.

You could do worse than to build consensus and agreement on definitions and names of the concepts in this chapter to establish your language of business design.

---

6   *Kevin Slavin: How Algorithms Shape Our World*, http://www.ted.com/talks/kevin_slavin_how_algorithms_shape_our_world.html (video), accessed 10 March 2012.

In the world of the semantic web,[7] customers can find products and suppliers can find customers with reducing human intervention. In a fast-moving global marketplace, communication has to be efficient to achieve agility; swimming against that tide, growing organizations face growing problems of information being 'lost in translation' as it passes between more and more people. To enable computerized and better human communication, it is fast becoming a necessity to create and/or adopt formally controlled language through corporate glossaries, thesauruses, taxonomies and ontologies.

To summarize: this category is about recognizing and establishing the information infrastructure required to run the business. Typically, the following elements form this category:

- *information domains*, to group together;

- *information entities* of common affinity;

- *information entity life histories;*

- *information sources* from which information may be supplied;

- *information stores;*

- *glossaries;*

- *taxonomies;*

- *ontologies* for those requiring more advanced management of semantics.

TIMING

One failure of business architecture practices is focusing on processes and services without explicitly understanding the timing factors that may make or break a business model. For example, understanding how the cycles of production synchronize with sales cycles and cash income is critical to managing cash flow and inventory. Analysing the two separately would be unlikely to reveal the existence or importance of the relationship. Timing is equally important in the marketplace: the basis of competitive advantage

---

7   http://en.wikipedia.org/wiki/Semantic_web, accessed 10 March 2012.

may be establishing a faster design-to-market product development life cycle. Without being cognizant of the frequency and timing with which competitors are releasing new customer offerings, there is a possibility of creating a business architecture that leaves the organization flat-footed.

Beyond the basic cycles, a critical factor is how resources of the organization are managed: seasonal, monthly, weekly, daily peaks and troughs can have a striking affect on supply and demand. Organizations can also be subject to immutable events, for example Year 2000, the Olympics, the introduction of new legislation or regulation, and so on. Capturing these explicitly is critical to ensure they are factored into the timelines of programmes of business change.

We have identified the following key elements composing this category:

- *business cycles*

- *trends*

- *world events*

These should be qualified and quantified to ensure their useful application in the architecture.

ORGANIZATION

We have identified the following key elements composing this category:

- *external organizations* (for example, commercial, non-commercial, governmental, suppliers, partners, consumer groups, industry bodies)

- *internal organization units*

- *roles*

- *groups of individuals* (for example, boards and committees)

- *skills*

- *competencies*

If there are specific external organizations influencing how the organization operates or plans to operate – for example, a specific regulator, your bank or a key supplier – then they should be captured as agents within the business architecture. If there are classes of organization – organizations playing specific roles in your marketplace, such as distributors or retail outlets – they should also be captured as agents. It should be possible to illustrate how each of these parties plays a role in the supply chain and channel to market.

It may not be possible to complete this picture without capturing individuals and the roles they play: external to the organization – for example as customers – and internally, in specific job positions – for example, the CEO or the CFO – or in generic roles, like a call centre agent. To define segment strategy, it is also necessary to capture as agents the key *customer profiles*.

ARCHETYPES AND INSTANCES

Some methodologies state that architecture should only be concerned with archetypes rather than instances of architectural elements: for example, *kinds* of product, *classes* of product, *types* of customer and *categories* of service. We say: 'Why fight with one hand behind your back?' To create an implementable architecture, it is sometimes necessary to focus on specific instances.

In the case of this category, if there is one organization that bears over your organization – for example, a regulator – explicitly identify both the archetype and the instance. If you need to define policy based upon region, then identify the specific regions within your location elements.

See also the 'Ontologies' section in Chapter 11.

In defining the mechanics of decision-making and governance within the organization, it is also necessary to capture groups of individuals as agents in order to recognize the existence of internal bodies that live in parallel to the organizational structure. Examples of these include the board of directors, investment boards and change control boards.

The critical skills and competencies required of your human resources to support your business model should be captured. Many organizations claim their businesses are based on the people, in which case, be clear about the kinds of people you require and the skills and competencies they should possess.

FINANCIAL

To understand the business model, it is necessary to capture the kinds of revenue stream and cost structure that will drive the finances of the business. Financial information is a facet of the operational business, so it is better not to replicate too much detail within the business architecture.

There is a case for defining some information at the higher levels of the architecture. Absolute financial measures are useful, especially if the business architecture is going to contain an in-depth financial model. For lighter-weight financial data, relative measures such as ratios and percentages are easier to manage over time, and they also avoid some of the sensitivities that occur with absolute numbers.

Although maintaining financial information at the lower levels of the business architecture makes less sense, there is a case for capturing limited information at the Macro and Strategic levels. Two examples illustrate this point. Firstly, understanding the proportion of fixed costs versus variable costs can provide input into how business architecture may be used to reduce the *operating leverage*. Secondly, without basic financial information, a trade-off decision between one architecture option and another may be invalid. We cannot escape the financials, and clearly there will be sensitivity around certain numbers, but that does not mean they should not be included in the architecture. After all, they represent a key category of input for the organizational design.

We have identified the following key elements composing this category:

- *revenue stream*

- *cost structure*

We would expect more specific financial data to be peppered across many of the elements listed elsewhere in this chapter.

LOCATION

To many businesses, *location* is a critical dimension to the business architecture. The supply chain, the locale of value creation, and the distribution network through which products and services are delivered to customers may all be subject to considerations of location.

There are different kinds of location to consider, depending on the business sector and line of business:

- The proximity and obstacles of physical geography (land, sea and air) can affect the supply of raw materials and the provisioning of physical products and 'in-person' services to customers.

- Political sovereignty, legal jurisdictions, tax jurisdictions and economic zones, and the boundaries within and between them can hinder or ease the value chain.

- Other, more specific locations subject to natural disasters can affect business continuity provisioning.

Locations can be managed in top-down composition hierarchies, and can also be grouped into clusters to suit other purposes to represent, for example, markets, sales regions or customer demographics.

We have identified the following key elements composing this category:

- *location* (which can be decomposed into other locations);

- *location type* (for example, geographical, political, legal, tax, economic, risk);

- *zone* (representing clusters or groups of locations, for example, markets and risk zones).

MATERIALS, CONSUMABLES AND BY-PRODUCTS

If your business is working in the energy exploration, aggregates, mining, fishing or agricultural industries, then elements to represent kinds of *raw material* and *source* will most likely feature in the business architecture.

The energy industry is interested in oilfields and wells, the agricultural industry is interested in land for arable and livestock production, the fishing industry is interested in fishing grounds, and so on.

In the process of value creation, every business expends some kind of consumable indirectly: agriculture consumes fertilizer, the paper industry consumes chemicals, and most businesses consume paper, water and power. The vast majority of organizations also generate carbon dioxide emissions as a by-product.

With environmental concerns and the increasing associated regulation, understanding the by-products of trading is becoming progressively more important. Already, carbon emissions and carbon footprints have entered the commercial vernacular. Corporate sustainability extends into environmental concerns, and already LEED (Leadership in Energy and Environmental Design) provides 'building owners and operators a concise framework for identifying and implementing practical and measurable green building design, construction, operations and maintenance solutions'.[8]

Typically, the following building blocks form this category:

- *consumables*

- *by-products*

- *raw materials*

- *sources*

The availability of an industry-specific classification system can enrich the definition of these elements.

The Technology Employed

It so often seems that information technology, such as the Internet, digital media and social networking, grabs the limelight. Where business architecture has been practised as part of business architecture, the IT-centric legacy has

---

8   http://en.wikipedia.org/wiki/Leadership_in_Energy_and_Environmental_Design, accessed 10 March 2012.

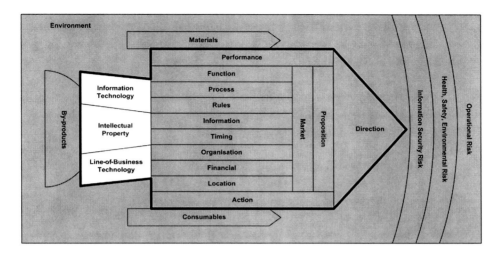

Figure 10.6   The technology employed

often meant that the wider world of technology receives little attention. In this group of categories we redress the balance and present a more rounded view, with architectural elements relating to:

- *information technology*

- *intellectual property*

- *line-of-business technology*

These are described below.

INFORMATION TECHNOLOGY

Without straying into IT architecture, the purpose of this category is to provide a consumer's view of IT, not a supplier's or manufacturer's view. From a business perspective, it is sufficient to recognize what the IT does and how it is used. Like driving a car, most of the time the driver sees the dashboard and instrumentation and knows that the car can transport them from A to B. The driver doesn't need to know how many horsepower or what torque the engine inside has. However, they may want to know the passenger capacity, the vehicle range and the fuel consumption, how much space there is for luggage, the frequency of service intervals and the proximity to the nearest service garage. These are all output specifications of function and quality, and this is the extent of how we describe information technology building blocks for the business architecture.

For the purposes of creating a complete business architecture, we would expect only the key equipment or facilities to be recognized as they relate to IT. In terms of equipment, this might include kinds of:

- fixed devices (for example, desktop computers);

- mobile devices (for example, tablets and laptops, PDAs);

- input devices (for example, keyboards, scanners, movement detectors);

- output devices (for example, printers, signage, broadcast screens).

In terms of facilities, the category could include:

- data centres;

- networks;

- key business applications;

- communication platforms for enabling channels to market, such as websites, email, social networking sites and so on.

INTELLECTUAL PROPERTY (IP)

'Intellectual property' refers to a number of distinct types of creations of the mind for which a set of exclusive rights is recognized, as well as the corresponding fields of law. Under intellectual property law, owners are granted certain exclusive rights to a variety of intangible assets, such as:

- musical, literary and artistic works;

- discoveries and inventions;

- words, phrases, symbols and designs.

Common types of intellectual property include:

- copyrights

- trademarks

- patents

- industrial design rights

- trade secrets (in some jurisdictions)[9]

In addition to those listed above, we would include *brands* and significant *legal contracts* as two more major classes.

It makes sense to recognize the growing importance of intellectual property building blocks within the business architecture. Increasingly, the exploitation of IP is becoming a major revenue stream. Organizations are also collaborating with agents outside the organization to develop new IP. Since the breadth of IP can be wide and varied, it is essential to establish your own classifications for IP.

LINE-OF-BUSINESS TECHNOLOGY

We have coined the term *line-of-business technology* (or alternatively, industry technology) to draw emphasis to the fact that almost every industry employs its own kind of technology. We have not called it 'non-IT' because we have to recognize the fact that, increasingly, line-of-business technology is connected, controlled and configured using information technology: hardware is now controlled by software.

We divide line-of-business technology into two kinds of architectural element:

- *equipment*

- *facilities*

---

9   http://en.wikipedia.org/wiki/Intellectual_property, accessed 10 March 2012.

Equipment represents any kind of machinery or device that is used to support the value chain that can be transported. *Facilities* represent any kind of plant, building or place where value-creation, transformation, storage of inventory or supply of services and goods takes place.

Here are a few examples of industries and some of their technological equipment and facilities:

- The petroleum sector uses oil and gas rigs, tankers, pipelines, pumps, refineries, pump stations, storage and petrol stations.

- The military uses radio, radar, satellites, ships, submarines, naval bases, barracks, tanks, airplanes and air bases.

- The utilities sector uses power stations, power grids, sub-stations and smart meters.

- The retail sector uses warehousing, delivery logistics, retail stores, RFID and point of sale.

- The telecommunications sector uses: cable networks, wireless transmission networks, wired networks, satellite networks, receivers, SIM cards and handsets.

- Most organizations use offices.

Each specific industry may need to create a lightweight taxonomy to qualify the facilities and equipment building blocks that are important.

Risks to the Business

As the world shrinks and global travel increases, the potential for a failure to extend geographically and create a domino effect increases year by year. Whether concerned with public health, the environment, financial markets or civil liberties, compliance and regulation is a growth business. Compounding this, as organizations operate with more open boundaries, physical security threats are being dwarfed by greater information security threats from cyberspace as well as from within. The threats are asymmetric, and a risk-based approach is required to ensure economically affordable solutions are deployed.

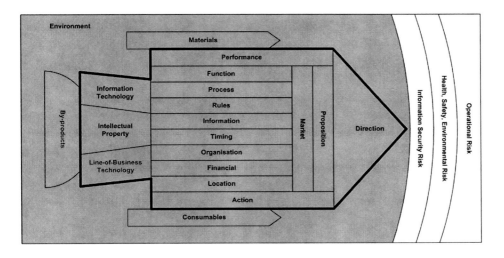

Figure 10.7   Risks to the business

The need to understand the major risk factors in the business architecture design is obvious, as evidenced by numerous very public failures in some of the world's largest organizations.

Within this category, we extend the concept of influence to cover specific classes of potential influence. For those businesses to which risk is a prominent issue, we have outlined three major specialized categories of risk:

- *health, safety and environmental risk*

- *operational risk*

- *information security risk*

Since the concepts of risk are largely the same, with just the classifications being specialized, we have identified the following kinds of building block:

- *risk;*

- *response (retain, transfer, reduce, prevent);*

- the *means of detection;*

- the kinds of *environment* where risks manifest.

The availability of an industry-specific classification system can enrich the definition of these elements.

HEALTH, SAFETY AND ENVIRONMENTAL RISK

For those organizations involved in operational activity that may cause harm, loss of life (to staff or the public at large) or destruction of the environment, the business is likely to be highly focused on the issues of health, safety and the environment. It is likely to manage these risks through adoption of:

- specific culture

- policy

- rigorous process and procedural controls

These issues can have a significant influence on design of the business, so understanding the key risks and recommended responses is important. The kinds of risk and response (whether they be the means of eliminating or reducing risk or monitoring, detecting and responding to unpreventable risks), should be captured as building blocks. Again, we are not trying to capture each and every actual risk, just establishing the key classifications so that the other parts of the business architecture can factor them into the business design as necessary.

OPERATIONAL RISK

As any compliance officer in the financial sector will testify, risk management and compliance has become almost an industry in itself. The financial sector has become such a complex, inter-connected, global web of organizations, instruments and contracts, that the need to guard against specific types of risk has become paramount. Without going into the detail of Basel 1, 2 or 3, a taxonomy of risk categories has been established to help guard against market or organization failure.

The list of risk categories of operational risk includes:

- *people* – human errors, fraud, inexperience and so on;

- *processes and procedures* – events, timings, durations and so on;

- *information technology* – business applications and infrastructure;

- *line-of-business technology* – machinery, transportation and so on.

Such risks exist within and outside the organization.

INFORMATION SECURITY RISK

As information technology becomes more pervasive within businesses and consumer products, the need to protect information and manage intellectual property and rights becomes paramount.

Information security and the associated industry standards, such as the ISO/IEC 27000 series,[10] is a discipline in its own right and is beyond the scope of this book. Nevertheless, we acknowledge the importance of this topic as a part of, and in relation to, business architecture. Information security is becoming an increasingly important aspect of IT, and the teams involved represent key partners and contributors to the business architecture, especially with regard to achieving business continuity.

Conclusion

When defining a business architecture, there may be a significant amount of information to capture to ensure that the correct architecture is developed and that it is complete. Gathering this data may seem daunting, but there is hope. Much of this information is likely to be living somewhere in the organization – certainly information that relates to the current state.

In many cases, you may find that different parts of the organization have defined and are maintaining information about the agents and building blocks outlined above. This is great news, as they are likely to have the authority to own and manage that information: Compliance departments often manage classifications of risk; Corporate Real Estate departments classify types of building and facility; Procurement departments categorise and manage acquisition of direct and indirect goods, services and resources. The next job is to formally enrol those groups, to legitimize them as the keepers of that part of the truth, and to harness it within your architecture.

---

10 http://www.iso.org/iso/search.htm?qt=ISO%2FIEC+27000&searchSubmit=Search&sort=rel&ty
pe=simple&published=on, accessed 10 March 2012.

Critical to capturing and maintaining information in your business architecture is to keep it *lean*, *definitive* and *key*. Keep the information lean, remembering that the architecture only needs to capture the essence of the information and can always refer out to supporting information better held elsewhere. Keep the information definitive, to ensure that there is only one source of the truth. If a situation arises where competing authorities crop up, then both will be compromised. Ownership and governance of the key elements is critical. Keeping the architecture focused on key information is fundamental. An approach we recommend is that for every category of architectural elements captured, there should always be a special element to represent the 'insignificant' others, either as a representative of or as a replacement for elements you do not wish to capture or have yet to do so.

> *The beginning of knowledge is the discovery of something we do not understand.*
>
> *Frank Herbert*

11

Building Views of the Organization

The Need for Architecture Views

In Chapter 10 we presented the primitive elements of a business architecture. Their explicit definition and cataloguing establishes the basis for a 'single version of the truth' that can be promulgated throughout the organization, to establish a common model and unify the thinking of the management and staff.

When looking at all the different kinds of element, the subject of business architecture can look a little dry, and maybe even impotent. A frequently posed challenge is: 'So what? Where's the value in that?'

The reality of large organizations is that the task of defining the semantics of these elements (and thereby creating a common language for business leaders and managers) is non-trivial. Standards groups continue to synergize the disparate concepts and evolving theories into a cohesive set of business architecture standards. The magnitude of the task becomes apparent for anyone who has tried. For most organizations it doesn't usually take long to realize how many differing opinions there are, how many different motivations there are, and how may egos need to be massaged just to assemble the lists of architectural elements necessary to describe the business. The soft skills of a business architect need to be refined and well tuned to achieve the consensus necessary to establish a sustainable business architecture. It also requires executive sponsorship to ensure that all the necessary stakeholders participate.

However, once these elements have been established (even a partial set), and using tooling to help, a model of valuable views of the business can be built very rapidly. As we demonstrate below, these views can be simple or complex, independent or combined. Without needing to wade through pages of verbose content, which is often boilerplate that carries little meaning, it is possible to quickly grasp the essence of the business in clear, discrete terms and with hard numbers as necessary.

Architecture in One Dimension

Beyond the basic capture of names of the architecture elements listed in Chapter 10, there is value in capturing attributes of these elements to build up and enrich 'the organizational story'. There are likely to be attributes common and specific to each kind of element. For example:

- What is the required availability ('hours of business') for each channel?

- What is the target lead time for product manufacture/supply?

- What is the target duration of the product development life cycle?

- What is the business contingency for a business function?

- How many staff are required in each business function?

The value of a simply defined and definitive list is better than the dozens of competing lists that can exist in many large organizations.

Architecture in Two Dimensions

We have also shown that once these elements have been established, they can be combined to answer more interesting questions that help determine how best to organize the business. For example:

- What products are to be sold through which channels?

- Which products are to be sold into which markets?

- What are the decision rights for each governance body?

- What taxation applies to what products?

- What regulation applies to what processes?

- What processes differ by country?

As well as providing simple yes/no answers, the matrices can be used to provide even more useful data at the point of intersection. For example:

- What is the target volume of product sales for each region by channel?

- What is the target volume percentage of customer revenue by customer segment?

In effect, establishing these simple matrices is creating relationships between elements, and these relationships can be loaded with attributes necessary to answer key questions, or define management intent and policy.

Architecture in Three Dimensions and Beyond

On the cost side of a business there are often questions like: 'What is the transaction cost in location Y? Is it cheaper than in location X?' Global businesses (that are chasing labour arbitrage savings through offshoring) are keen to understand the cost of similar transactions in each trading location to help identify opportunities for savings. Answering the question involves bringing together multiple elements in a multi-dimensional matrix:

Product Being Sold/Serviced × Transaction Type × Location and Cost of the Labour × The Market of the Customer

As a further example, defining a market participation strategy for global business would need to combine Market × Customer Segment to articulate where to trade, and then specify how to reach the customers within the markets by adding the further dimensions of Customer Offering and Channel. Of course, the Customer Offering may already be hard-wired to Customer Segment in a Customer Segment × Customer Offering matrix. At the intersection of this multi-dimensional matrix, management intent and policy can be expressed as necessary; revenue targets and customer acquisition targets can also be specified.

Complicating the matter further, the time dimension may be added to any of these matrices, to indicate how the picture changes over time.

Beyond Matrices

In the previous section we may have laboured the use of matrices, but that is because almost everyone is familiar with spreadsheets to some degree. Maybe with more effort and a more aesthetically pleasing and simpler format, the same data and relationships can be conveyed using different kinds of diagram, chart and heatmap.

The Business Model Canvas approach provides an example of how different views of business architecture are brought together on one page. The positioning of what the various authors call building blocks (that we call *views*) are presented spatially on a page showing the supply chain and the cost/revenue sides of the business. Using overlay techniques, as we have demonstrated in our Business Model Canvas (see Appendix 3), it is possible to illustrate rich and powerful relationships: for example, showing which customer segments are targeted by each customer offering and what revenue that generates. The scope for building up the elements and relationships into ever-richer representations is endless, so caution must be exercised to ensure enthusiasm doesn't overtake necessity – perhaps by applying the Pareto principle.[1]

Taxonomies

Another key form of relationship used within architecture is one that indicates whether one element is more general than another – a *generalization taxonomy*. We have mentioned a lot about organization and classification – the subject of taxonomies. These taxonomies are in essence hierarchical organizations similar to an organogram. In Chapter 1, we presented a small taxonomy of terms that we have used in this book.

Well-constructed taxonomies become powerful tools to define and communicate concepts and terms with brevity and precision. The leaves of the hierarchy (imagining an upside-down tree) are normally concrete things that might be recognizable in the real world. The branches are essentially

---

1   http://en.wikipedia.org/wiki/Pareto_principle, accessed 10 March 2012.

generalizations of the things below them. Designing large taxonomies is a skill, but once developed, they can be helpful in two ways:

1. They provide clear semantics like a dictionary, so that everyone can communicate clearly and ambiguously.

2. Utilizing the abstract elements can dramatically reduce verbosity, ambiguity and confusion. If you read the words 'customer offering' in this book, because we have said that this represents a generalization of 'products' and 'services', we don't have to keep writing 'products and/or services'.

Taxonomies are everywhere, and they are valuable in improving internal communication and dialogue with suppliers and customers. After all, how would marketeers exist if they were not able to create another product category to differentiate the customer proposition or another customer segment to refine marketing activity?

So taxonomies are a powerful means to describe parts of the architecture of business. As we mentioned above, they can be used to classify a variety of elements, such as: Benefit Types, Measurement Types, Location Types, Terms, Products, Services, Customers, Channels, Organizations, Roles, Revenue Streams, Cost Structures and Technology. They can be used to capture and define target standard building blocks of the business around which standardization and rationalization initiatives can be driven and measured. Put another way: stopping short of quantities, taxonomies can represent the bill of materials (the raw materials, subassemblies, intermediate assemblies, sub-components, components and parts) required to create business capability or customer offerings.

These taxonomies should be specified at the Strategic level, and utilized in the lower Programme and Project levels of the architecture. The governance processes around these programmes and projects would use these standardized building blocks to measure how proposed solutions conform to the required standards.

Generalization taxonomies are not the only way to describe the architecture hierarchical. A *composition hierarchy*, such as a bill of materials (BOM), can be used to describe necessary sub-components to make an assembly. The hierarchical nature means that parts can be assembled into subassemblies, subassemblies into assemblies, and assemblies into final products. An organization structure presented using an organogram is presenting a composition hierarchy.

Ontologies

Ontologies are an extension of taxonomies, but rather than just focusing on the classifications of things, they can also include real instances. To illustrate: where as a taxonomy of locations may include 'Free Trade Area', an ontology may contain, for example, the EU and NAFTA as instances of 'Free Trade Area', as shown in Figure 11.1.

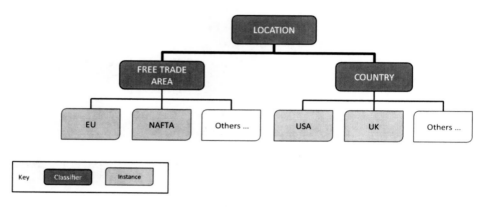

Figure 11.1   Example ontology

Some real instances of things can dominate areas of business operation. Recognizing these definitively provides a foundation for defining business rules, policies, processes and so on. The involvement of specific countries and trade areas drives specific rules for taxation, importation and exportation, to name a few.

There are specialist tools that enable the creation and management of taxonomies and ontologies.

Blueprints

The generalization taxonomy and composition hierarchy create static views of the architecture, but they do not convey how the parts of the organization physically or logically fit together. They do not convey the inter-connections between the parts. Furthermore, they do not convey the dynamics of how the parts and connectors, once assembled, work together.

For what we are calling the *blueprints* of how the parts fit together and how the parts work together, there are many specialized (and sometimes competing) notations and diagrammatic standards: for example, BPMN competes with EPC and UML for Business Process Modelling. A key point to establish as part of the language for the business architecture is which notations and styles you are going to adopt. CEOs and business managers don't want to see the same kind of information presented differently each time. They don't have time to learn complex notations, let alone multiple competing notations. Furthermore, if you are architecting different parts of your organization in parallel or at different times, you don't want one team using the equivalent of a metric standards and another team using the equivalent of the imperial standard. This happened to NASA in September 1999, when it lost its $125 million Mars Climate Orbiter probe due to different teams using different standards.[2] You need the same language and semantics, as we mentioned above. Establishing a catalogue of views with examples and styles is an important task in increasing the maturity of an architecture practice.

And finally, a note to those who may be engaged with process modelling: make sure your IT team is bought into the notation and tooling to minimize any transformation necessary to create software specifications or configure business process automation platforms.

> *Science is facts; just as houses are made of stones, so is*
> *science made of facts; but a pile of stones is not a house*
> *and a collection of facts is not necessarily science.*
> *Henri Poincaré*

---

2   'Metric mishap caused loss of NASA orbiter', CNN Tech (30 September 1999), http://articles. cnn.com/1999-09-30/tech/9909_30_mars.metric.02_1_climate-orbiter-spacecraft-team-metric-system?_s=PM:TECH, accessed 10 March 2012.

PART V
Practising Business Architecture

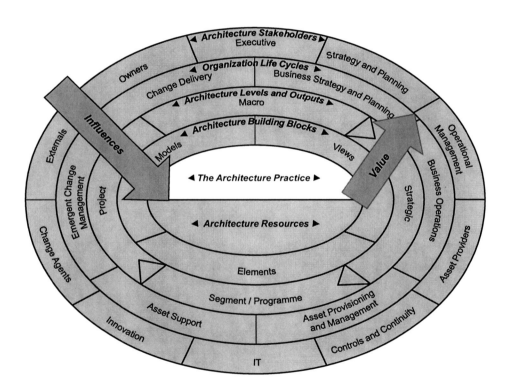

12

Overcoming the Barriers to Business Architecture

The Stigma of Business Architecture

Business architecture is a relatively new discipline, and like any new discipline, the risk of failure is high. Arguably, the closest comparison is enterprise architecture, which although displaying signs of maturity and stability, has shown that it can be a tough nut to crack, with many aborted attempts in its wake. And many of those that have survived live on do so with some prominent scars; winning trust and credibility can take months or sometimes years, but it can be lost in days or hours.

A traditional perception of architecture in general is that it is theoretical, with architects sitting in 'ivory towers', so there is a need to adopt a value delivery mindset to ensure successful execution. Architects are quite often deep thinkers, but they also need to execute and think about the delivery of architecture from their customer's perspective.

Business architecture is intended to support the management and evolution of organizations – it aims to break down complexity through the application of holistic analysis and design techniques. With business architecture, you can understand complexity, position for change and enhance value creation. These themes must act as touchstones for a business architecture practice.

Business architecture is not to be practised in isolation; it is not a one-off process; it needs to be woven into the fabric of the organization. In Chapter 7 we illustrated the opportunities for weaving the business architecture practice into this fabric through the various life cycles found within an organization. But doing so requires the removal of various barriers. In this chapter we look at a worst case scenario and then move on to discuss the kinds of barriers facing business architects which need to be overcome or avoided as part of engaging within the wider organization.

Worst Case Scenario

Many established architecture practices constantly face an uphill battle to justify their existence. They often operate on the sidelines, and when they do participate in change initiatives, often it is too late in the process. The net effect of this is that architecture is seen as an expensive, ineffective and low-performing function that does not add value. Many architects may have experienced scenarios where their function is ostensible in nature, with no hard remit or authority to engage with the stakeholders it needs to engage with. Architecture practices are often perceived as ivory towers disconnected from reality. The architects are seen as too theoretical and insufficiently pragmatic. It seems that unlike other functions, the requirement to justify its existence comes around far too often for many practising architects. Without doubt, the wider industry accepts that architecture is a good thing and that any serious company should establish a team. The problem lies with the fact that the generation of C-suite leaders struggles to understand why. Some architecture practices exist because it fits the trend.

The picture painted above is perhaps an extreme one. However, it illustrates the point that understanding how to deliver value remains tantalizingly out of reach for many architects. In our experience, re-examination of value comes very much down to how the architecture practice sets out its stall and how architects connect with other parts of the organization.

To understand these problems, first we must open the lens to consider a fuller set of factors that can form barriers to establishing a business architecture practice.

Barriers

Business architecture is no easy ride. If it is to deliver on its promise, there are numerous barriers to overcome – for individual business architects and for business architecture practices. The main barriers are shown in Figure 12.1.

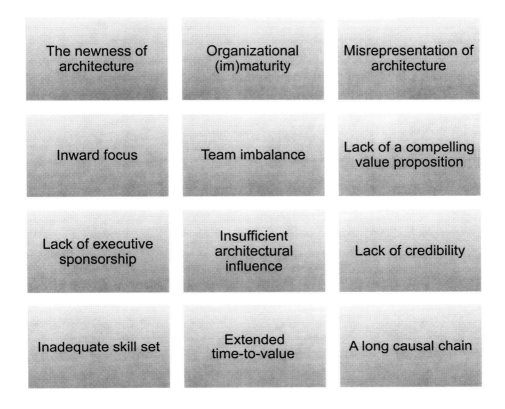

Figure 12.1   Business architecture barriers

We will take a brief look at each of these barriers in the sections below.

NEWNESS OF ARCHITECTURE

We have to accept that business architecture is a relatively new discipline and that many organizations have a relatively undeveloped knowledge or understanding of the discipline. That is not to say that some of the activities and methods did not exist before 'business architecture' was recognized as a discipline in its own right; developing blueprints, operating models and capability models, for example, is not new to today's businesses, it's just that they were often produced under different names. As business architecture does not yet feature heavily on graduate or post-graduate business administration course curricula, architects have to accept that before formal operations can commence, appropriate training and education is required to ensure the rationale and purpose of business architecture is understood by stakeholders. Alongside the requisite competencies and skills, there needs to be a framework, be it formal or informal, with supporting facilities as necessary (such as tools) with which to operate. As business architecture is still in its infancy and its role and position have yet to stabilize, it is easy for business architecture to be seen as confusing.

ORGANIZATIONAL (IM)MATURITY

Coupled with the newness of the discipline, the act of applying 'architectural thinking and practices' does represent a new way of working: new methods, techniques and disciplines (choose your own words). To achieve sponsorship, architects need to convince management that existing ways of working are hindering performance and that the proposed alternative will improve performance. Despite Albert Einstein eloquently describing insanity as 'doing the same thing over and over again and expecting different results', organizations repeatedly utilize change methodologies that often fail to deliver predictable outcomes and the envisaged benefits. At a time when organizations are segmented into silos, each with its own opportunities and pressures, identifying synergies for the greater good – promoting strategic over tactical initiatives – and looking beyond the immediate budget cycle is challenging.

It requires a certain level of personal and professional maturity in the members of the management team to acknowledge that change is necessary, or at the very least worth running a trial to investigate. It takes strong individuals to recognize that the organization is 'failing', challenge the status quo, champion the cause and act as advocate for a new approach. One of the first missions of a business architect may be to find that individual to kick-start an architecture practice.

MISREPRESENTATION OF ARCHITECTURE

We hear all too often questions that demonstrate a fundamental misunderstanding and misrepresentation of architecture. How do I deliver value from my architecture project? How do I justify my architecture project? The inquisitors are missing the point. Maybe the way in which TOGAF's Architecture Development Method (ADM) is executed has been misinterpreted. Architecture is a means to an end, not an end in itself. Architecture projects do not exist. Change programmes and change projects exist. They exist to affect a change in the capabilities of the organization. Even setting up an architecture practice is not really an architecture project. It is just another business change project establishing a new business capability: an architecture capability. Therefore, the proposition and benefits of an architecture set-up project should be described in terms of business outcomes as they relate to and create value for the wider business. The bottom line is this: architecture must be woven into existing change life cycles.

INWARD FOCUS

Another feature sometimes exhibited by architecture practices is an obsession with internal capability and tooling. As a means to an end, architecture practitioners should think and behave like business people. They need to provide services that add value, so they need to focus on how to engage, with whom they engage, and how they help their 'customers' achieve their objectives.

Building an architectural model or assets that cannot be applied in the delivery of value is an exercise in waste. Therefore, if tooling is required, the cost of acquisition and deployment will have to be justified through a business case like any other investment.

TEAM IMBALANCE

In addition to the internal focus, we have often come across architecture practices full of only architects. Architects are usually great thinkers, but it is a rare breed that is able to operate outside its normal comfort zone for long periods. To be successful, the architecture practice must have balance. With reference to Belbin's work[1] on team theory, we cannot recommend highly enough that your practice include members who can operate across the range of roles required to create a high-performing team. In Belbin's terms, you need plants, monitor-evaluators, resource investigators, co-ordinators, shapers, team workers, implementers, completer finishers, and maybe some specialists.

LACK OF A COMPELLING VALUE PROPOSITION

What we are advocating is the development of a business plan, just like when setting up any other business or a unit within a business. The business plan should provide a financial model and an illustration of how your customers

---

1   http://en.wikipedia.org/wiki/Meredith_Belbin, accessed 10 March 2012.

and the organization will benefit. It should also include some kind of *benefits realization plan*. It should be clear how business architects will be funded, how they should book their time, and how they will cross-charge their services. The smaller the architecture team, the lighter the weight of plan required.

For those setting up an architecture practice or just beginning to practise architecture for the first time, establishing a value proposition is perceived as a daunting and even impossible challenge. Anyone who has spent time trawling the Internet, research groups, industry bodies, finding case studies with hard numbers will have found that they have yielded few or zero results. It may be that anecdotal evidence is available, and we believe that it is important to capture and leverage your own anecdotes. However, anecdotes don't fire up those with an eye on finances.

As entrepreneurs will testify, investors demand that a clear business model be defined. It is unlikely that you will be required to demonstrate how to make a profit, but the following questions should be at the forefront of your mind:

- What are you selling?

- What need are you satisfying?

- Who are your target customers?

- Can you deliver the proposition at a price customers will be prepared to pay?

- Can you deliver the proposition at a quality customers are prepared to accept?

- Can you deliver the proposition at acceptable service levels?

- Finally, why should they buy from you and nobody else?

If architectural activity is fragmented across the organization, can you sell the benefits of consolidating those resources and activities under one team?

Maybe this all sounds too much. But if you haven't done this before, it's probably good practice to try. After all, as business architects, it is likely you will be involved in similar activities for the larger business you work within.

Unless you wish to remain in a facilitatory role, having experience of doing it yourself will build your confidence and help you to build credibility with your customers and get involved as partners in change in the future.

LACK OF EXECUTIVE SPONSORSHIP

Senior management will be driven by numbers and value creation. The creation of a business plan and a demonstration of cause and effect will enable your desired sponsors to understand how the activities of architecture fit with and affect the wider organization. Not only will this enable senior management to understand, it will also enable the partners that architects rely upon to implement the architecture and deliver your value. Another useful tool to develop is your 'elevator pitch', but be careful, as you have many stakeholders, so you are likely to need different pitches for different elevators.

Furthermore, without executive sponsorship, invitations to parties are harder to come by. Business architects need to participate early, when organizations are taking the longer-term view (spanning budget cycles), when the business strategy is being formulated. Business architects need to be able to understand the strategy so that they can articulate it and reflect it in their business architecture.

INSUFFICIENT ARCHITECTURAL INFLUENCE

Many architectures may be plausible from a theoretical perspective. However, too often the theory doesn't translate into tangible results. The architect's diagrams remain as slideware; the only measure that can be associated with them is what it cost to produce them. (As somebody once said: 'The only operating system on which the architecture could run is presentation software.')

For a business architecture practice to succeed, it needs to be integrated into the change processes of the organization, not an independent or one-off process. As we discussed in Chapters 6 and 7, there is a need to understand stakeholders and the life cycles of change; without that understanding, architecture is often seen as having little, if any, added value, and hence architects get overlooked. Without stakeholder engagement, participation in the change life cycles and an appropriate governance framework, business architecture has limited influence within the organization.

LACK OF CREDIBILITY

To establish credibility, architects must recognize that they need strong practices of marketing, selling, stakeholder engagement, communication and performance management. Architects must quickly demonstrate empathy with stakeholders and an understanding of their business needs. This either requires in-depth understanding of the specific sector, or a breadth of experiences that transcend industries. The business plan provides only a platform, so architects, besides developing architecture, need to participate in the disciplines listed above. During the initial stages of practising architecture, it is important to maintain presence and visibility. When wins come, they must be communicated. It may not always be obvious that wins come because of architecture. Therefore, when they do come, be ready to demonstrate how architecture participated or acted as a catalyst.

In addition to demonstrating that architecture pays, the path to engage with customers in the business is often blocked by a third party that reduces the opportunities to connect directly and build that credibility. This may be observed in organizations where business architects are positioned within the IT function behind an IT relationship management team.

To overcome this hurdle, it pays to define what value you provide and why you are best to provide it. In a crowded marketplace you have to carve out a niche that is acceptable to the existing parties. In the IT relationship manager scenario, it may be that you are able to reduce the burden on the IT relationship manager and provide more in-depth analysis to the business practitioners the relationship manager deals with. The working relationship may not start out with direct contact, but as time goes by and trust in the relationship grows, these opportunities will surely arise.

INADEQUATE SKILL SET

One reason why credibility can be lacking is because business architects have inadequate skills to develop the architecture, engage with stakeholders and ultimately obtain value from their architectures. The role of architect demands a broad range of hard skills (business, engineering, technical and so on) and soft skills (interpersonal, motivational, communication, influencing and so on) that must be demonstrated at a range of levels within and outside the organization. Business architects need to know how to build business cases, develop benefit profiles and put forward compelling propositions.

While some skills can be acquired through formal training, seminars and conferences, there is no substitute for experience. Attempts to short-circuit the acquisition of experience often leave the practitioner in an exposed position, and any credibility gained can be quickly eroded.

Later in the chapter, we look at the role of the business architect and the competencies required to overcome this barrier.

A LONG CAUSAL CHAIN

The causal chain between developing architecture and realizing benefit from architecture is potentially lengthy. Once architecture has been defined, its application in the construction and deployment of one or more business solutions involves numerous individuals and groups. Between the architect and the recipient(s) of the solution, there is a possibility that the architecture is not executed to the letter, so some of the projected benefits may be lost. Even if followed to the letter, the architecture may not yield projected benefits. In addition, when it comes to claiming the benefits and proving the root cause, those parties involved in adopting the architecture may all be standing in line, closer to the results, ready to claim the benefits themselves. Double counting of benefits is a familiar sight.

EXTENDED TIME-TO-VALUE

Considerable time can elapse between 'doing' architecture and realizing the benefits of the architected business solution. Often, this time span will stretch over one or more financial planning periods. If you look backward, do you feel confident that you can claim that benefit, based on something you did two years ago, or one year ago? Organizations have short memories. If you look forward, do you think you can justify and measure benefits in two years' time that can be attributed to your architecture? This is where integrating the business architecture practice into the organization's change life cycle prevents its separation and/or a perception of disconnection.

Engagement Principles

Having considered the barriers that must be overcome, we will now take a more positive view of how business architecture as a practice can fulfil its value proposition. The experiences of many companies, colleagues and practising architects leads to a set of critical success factors (CSFs), or as we refer to them, *engagement principles*, as set out in Figure 12.2.

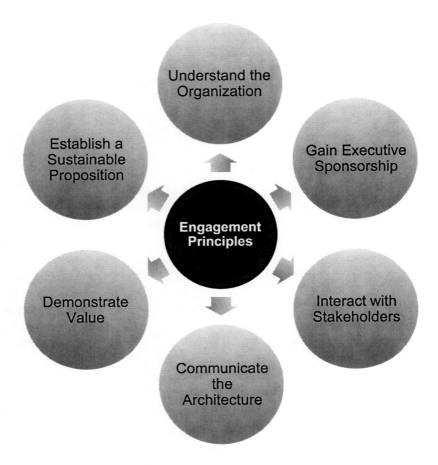

Figure 12.2   Engagement principles

We place equal emphasis on each of these principles. They are not mutually exclusive, nor are they exhaustive. This is not a process to be followed in a specific order; these principles apply continuously – constant change dictates this. They are points of reference with which to orientate and ensure engagement is successful.

The principles may seem obvious, but it is surprising how often they are overlooked, or addressed at a point in time rather than continuously, given that the organizational ecosystem is constantly changing.

UNDERSTAND THE ORGANIZATION

Understand the organization to which the business architecture applies or is to be applied. This includes, but is not necessarily limited to:

- its motivations and plans – its vision, mission, strategy, goals, objectives, value proposition and so on;

- its internal and external stakeholders – those who may influence or be influenced by the architecture, including (but not necessarily limited to) customers, suppliers, partners, regulators, industry bodies, media and so on;

- its competitors – including long-standing and emerging players;

- its key assets – the products it acquires, uses and produces, and the services it consumes and delivers;

- its key processes – the processes it executes to deliver its products and services;

- its change initiatives – the key investments it is making – that is, the programmes and projects that are planned or under way to move it towards its vision (although not all may contribute to the vision);

- its business cycles – the financial accounting, budget, trading, change and other cycles;

- its footprint – the offices, stores, outlets, channels and locations it has, the geographies that it covers, the customer base it has, and so on;

- its figures – revenues, expenditure, profit, and so on;

- its history and culture – its highs and lows, its acquisitions, its attitude towards its customers and staff.

To improve that understanding, useful resources to consider include the following (one on its own is unlikely to be sufficient):

- a business operating model – see Chapter 9;

- the business architecture classification system – see Chapter 10;

- the use of matrices and taxonomies – see Chapter 11;

- a Business Model Canvas – see Chapter 15;

- the Business Motivation Model – see Chapter 16;

- a RASCI matrix.

RACI VERSUS RASCI

We recommend the use of RASCI over RACI because in today's world of collaboration and social networking, achievements are rarely the result of one person's effort. One person may lead the work (Responsible), but often working closely with a team of collaborators and contributors (Supporting).

This principle does not imply that you document the entire organization in minute detail; it is about understanding the context – rows 1 and 2 of the Zachman Framework (see Chapter 15), for example. And even though the scope of a business architecture initiative may not be the entire organization, it is still worthwhile having a contextual and broad understanding at whatever level or segment you develop your architecture.

GAIN EXECUTIVE SPONSORSHIP

C-suite-level sponsorship comes in many forms:

- Funding – providing or securing funds for initial and longer term investment propositions.

- Owning – accepting accountability for the success (or failure) of architecture-led initiatives; empowering others to deliver.

- Championing – communicating and promoting the architecture-led initiatives; driving the necessary behaviours.

- Leading – establishing and/or supporting the vision; taking the initiative; establishing and nurturing teams: motivating individuals to share the vision and deliver the value.

- Supporting – providing support to those stakeholders who are responsible for establishing the architecture and delivering the value.

- Mentoring – providing education, support, problem-solving and motivational dimensions.

- Resolving – facilitating the resolution of issues; removing the obstacles that prevent progress and the delivery of value.

- Communicating – sharing the vision and the strategy to realize the vision.

An executive sponsor should own the business proposition for business architecture and manage the realization of benefits. Furthermore, a good executive sponsor will be challenging and demanding – requiring the architecture to be fit for purpose and tuned to deliver demonstrable value in a timely manner.

Architectures that are fuelled from the top down rather than from the bottom up tend to deliver more value more rapidly.

INTERACT WITH STAKEHOLDERS

This principle is about communicating, collaborating and co-operating with stakeholders within and outside the organization, not as a one-off activity, but on a continuous basis.

In the same way that a new business must establish itself in the market place, identify its customers, its investors, its partners, its suppliers and so on, so must an architecture practice. If an architecture practice is to claim the delivery of compelling products and services, it must ensure they are positioned well and differentiated from other similar offerings from elsewhere in the organization.

Stakeholder engagement relies on a range of behaviours, including the following:

- Invest in 360-degree relationships. Don't 'manage' stakeholders, interact with them – treat them as you would expect to be treated. Put yourselves in their shoes and listen to them.

- Gain consensus. 'Yes' in a meeting is one thing, demonstrable support is another. People often act differently if they have some responsibility for or interest in the outcome. In other words, get their skin in the game.

- Understand individual behaviour and motivation. Understand their motivation at a personal, career and role level (what's on their balanced scorecard or personal performance targets). Understanding this will leave you in good shape to leverage those relationships in good times, and especially in challenging times.

- Go native. Talk the talk. Speak the language of the stakeholders. Adopt the relevant metaphors.

- Interact with stakeholders early and regularly. Establish the business architecture with them, rather than trying to dictate it to them. If you have to, let them think it's their idea to do so. Collaborate and be seen to collaborate. This doesn't mean you have to be everyone's friend. You will still need to stand your ground too, when necessary and appropriate to do so.

All deep and enduring relationships provide mutual benefit. When either side feels lessening benefit, the relationship is likely to deteriorate. If there is one golden rule, make sure you factor reciprocity into your relationships, or they will die.

In large organizations, often the surest way to guarantee help and collaboration from stakeholder teams or individuals is to plan in a timely manner to ensure that whatever drives their performance incorporates objectives that facilitate the objectives of the business architecture practice. If your organization uses a BSC for performance appraisal, you can guarantee the collaboration of key influencers by securing an appropriate objective on their BSC. Such aspiration invariably involves the support of executive sponsors.

SOMETHING FOR EVERYONE AND NOTHING FOR ANYONE

From a CEO's perspective, a business architecture should resonate well, since it should take a holistic view of the business. The danger for those below the CEO, working in specific areas, is that the architecture is described in generalized terms which are too abstract or removed from their normal thinking: they believe there is nothing in it specifically for them. To mitigate this, it is essential to demonstrate the relationships between the generalized concepts and the specialized concepts with which they are familiar. Highlight opportunities and synergies and build a common language.

COMMUNICATE THE ARCHITECTURE

Underpinning stakeholder engagement is effective communication, gathering and disseminating information. Open and honest communication leads to greater trust and depth of relationships; it makes for lasting relationships. A British Telecommunications marketing campaign had the slogan 'It's good to talk,' and that is certainly true of business architecture – indeed, any architecture discipline. But it also pays to listen – and to be seen to listen. You should spend as much time fostering relationships (communicating, collaborating and co-operating) as you do defining, establishing, maintaining and implementing the business architecture.

Many C-suite executives and senior architects spend a significant amount of their time (as much as 50 per cent in some cases) on the road, not just communicating, but responding to concerns and opportunities, maintaining a dialogue that promotes trust and fosters long-term partnerships. All architects should invest in such communication.

All channels of communication are likely to be employed: face-to-face, email, telephone, the Web and paper, and each needs to be given the appropriate consideration to ensure that straightforward and consistent messages are delivered. One major mobile telephone operator has defined an internal standard and accompanying process that requires all architecture communication material to be reviewed before it is issued; it has to pass a 'tone of voice' test. Therefore, terms like 'meta model' have to be communicated in plain language, and they use icons on deliverables to show that that they have been approved by the relevant internal authority (Compliance, Security, Technology Forum and so on).

Many larger organizations[2] produce an Architecture Communications Plan as a formal artefact to ensure that:

- key stakeholders are identified and engaged;

- the media of communication are identified;

- a consistent communication process is applied;

- the key messages are communicated consistently;

- a feedback mechanism is established.

When everyone is singing from the same song sheet, the results resonate.

DEMONSTRATE VALUE

What you say is important, but what you *do* is more important. Deliver value; demonstrate the value you deliver. The right solution isn't always the perfect solution; you need the buy-in; you need to compromise.

We set out the value proposition of business architecture as being:

- better investment decisions;

- increased value for money;

- faster, lower-cost and more consistent delivery;

- reduced operational risk;

---

2   For example, see United States Department of Commerce Enterprise Architecture Program Support, *Enterprise Architecture Communications Plan Version 1.0* (2006), http://ocio.os.doc.gov/s/ groups/public/@doc/@os/@ocio/@oitpp/documents/content/prod01_004897.pdf, accessed 10 March 2012.

- improved agility;

- increased flexibility.

As we discussed in the section on barriers above, a long causal chain and time-to-value cloud the ability to make a direct link between architecture and the delivery of value.

To demonstrate that these values are being realized depends on having:

- effective measures;

- the mechanisms in place to take the measurements;

- a long enough timescale to obtain reliable results;

- the insight to interpret the results;

- the foresight to provide feedback about the results to inform the business architecture.

Few organizations today have an established benefits realization process that is independent of specific programmes, projects, people and organizational structure, that spans financial planning periods and links to the corporate vision and goals (for example, via a balanced scorecard). Typically, benefit realization is down to the vigilance of an individual who links adjacent budget cycles. Ideally, if a tactical investment decision is made, the business case should include the subsequent migration to the strategic solution within an appropriate timeframe – that is, it will go to the top of the list of the next budget cycle. This needs long-term executive sponsorship and determination.

There is a difference between 'delivering' and delivering value. Delivering value doesn't necessarily mean delivering projects – it is the responsibility of project managers to deliver projects. A project's delivery may be an enabler to a broader architectural benefit or business outcome. Value can come in many forms, for example:

- Providing a view of the organization that can identify opportunities for rationalisation, optimization and leverage.

- Bringing visibility dynamics and inter-dependencies within the organization to expose root cause problems.

- Enabling organizations to achieve strategic alignment, demonstrating traceability from intent (investment of financial and human capital) to outcome (faster time to market, reduced cost-to-market, reduced cost-in-market, longer time-in-market, customer satisfaction, shareholder satisfaction and so on).

- Providing a mechanism to balance risk with opportunity more effectively.

- Providing a better mechanism to undertake impact analysis of change and estimate cost of change and thus provide the ability to unearth hidden costs of change earlier.

Specific deliveries can help. Delivering a specific outcome can help to establish credibility, open doors and hence pave the way for further architecture initiatives. The architecture practice of a Canadian bank delivered a reusable 'Branch Locator' function that was available throughout the organization – a simple but effective function that demonstrated value to a broad range of stakeholders. Doors opened. There is nothing wrong with starting small.

Finally, stakeholder perspective is vital; not all stakeholders are able to, or are in a position to, see the bigger picture and the contribution that a specific initiative may be making to that bigger picture – hence the importance of nurturing stakeholder relationships.

ESTABLISH A SUSTAINABLE PROPOSITION

Business architecture should be part of the fabric of the organization, part of the fabric of the change process – not an independent process; not a one-off process. Architecture needs to be iterative, and so must the development cycles. Business architecture is a journey, not a destination – constant change determines that. Therefore:

- Embed business architecture into the delivery mechanisms – downstream.

- Embed business architecture into the business planning mechanisms – upstream.

The fundamental point here is that the major benefits in architecture come through long-term investment, and that business people deal in much shorter-term objectives and financial goals. For architecture to be effective and to survive the commercial pressures, it must make an impact on an ongoing basis and also take advantage of 'quick wins' along the way. It must be able to demonstrate the causality of architecture activities. Moreover, the relationship with the numerous architecture stakeholders must be cultivated and maintained over time. If nothing else, architects should ensure they have a strong grasp of the big picture. Merely possessing that picture means that you provide a unique perspective that no one else can provide; this in itself is demonstrating value.

As well as establishing strong foundations (the core business architecture artefacts such as principles, policies, standards, reference and other models), sustainability may also mean:

- managing risks and issues;

- resolving conflict and brokering solutions;

- overseeing quality;

- innovating (in terms of solutions and approaches to business architecture);

- responding proactively to change;

- establishing feedback loops and means of performance measurement.

Having a fine business architecture (however you perceive 'fine') does not guarantee value for your business.

Anyone who has never made a mistake has never tried anything new.

Albert Einstein

13

The Business Architect

The Business Architect Role

Given that there is no single universally agreed definition of what business architecture is (or architecture in general in the context of organizations), the role of business architect is somewhat elusive. The role tends to be relative to the organization (and more specifically the people within it who write the job specification). In some ways, everyone's an architect. Browsing through job descriptions in the marketplace, one could easily believe that a business architect has to be all things to all people. Many business architect role specifications describe a role that few individuals (if any) would be able to fulfil.

In Chapter 3 we identified four levels within an organization to which business architecture can be applied:

1. **Macro** – establishing the vision and desired target state and the benefits the organization brings to its stakeholders.

2. **Strategic** – supplementing the vision with target capabilities, supporting principles and policies and a current state environmental assessment to provide contextual rationale.

3. **Segment/programme** – translating the strategic activities into delivery-focused change initiatives at the segment or programme level.

4. **Project** – engaging with projects to communicate the architecture and oversee alignment to it.

A business architect may operate at one or more of these levels, although operating at all four is unlikely, especially in a large organization – time would not allow for it. Nevertheless, all levels are needed. Creating the vision is one thing; having the resources who understand the vision, understand what is necessary to make it happen and make it happen is another. The more mature the organization in terms of architecture, the higher the level at which the role exists.

Business architecture role specifications tend to vary depending on the level at which the role is expected to operate. However, the common denominators that should exist at all levels relate to the engagement principles discussed in Chapter 12:

- Understand the organization.

- Gain executive sponsorship.

- Interact with stakeholders.

- Communicate the architecture.

- Demonstrate value.

- Establish a sustainable proposition.

In addition, professional and personal development is necessary to ensure that skills and knowledge remain current. The pace of change we discussed in earlier chapters demands that architects ride the wave of change rather than get caught in its wake.

The typical core activities undertaken by a business architect are shown in Figure 13.1.

In Table 7.7 we mapped these architecture services to the various business life cycles (Strategic Planning, Programmes, Projects and so on). Business architects may also provide supporting activities; we have summarized these in Appendix 1, again showing a mapping to the various business life cycles.

There are many factors that can influence the execution of the role of business architect. Here are a few examples.

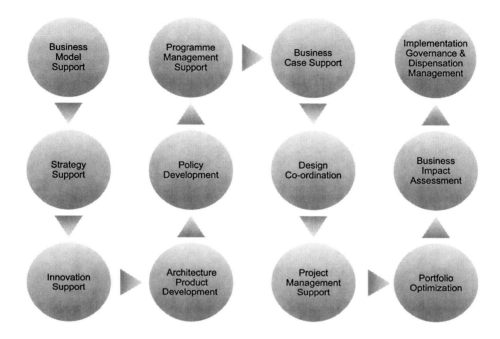

Figure 13.1   Business architecture core activities

THE TYPE OF INDIVIDUAL FULFILLING IT

The role can extend to the qualities and attributes of the architect. Great theoretical architects may not carry authority within an organization if they cannot connect with the C-suite players. Conversely a savvy, results-driven, business-knowledgeable strong communicator with gravitas doesn't necessarily have to have deep technical knowledge to be an influential player; an appreciation of the technology and an understanding of the opportunities, limitations and pitfalls of technology should be sufficient.

Business architects need to know how to build business cases, develop benefit profiles and put forward compelling propositions.

THE SIZE OF THE ORGANIZATION

Larger organizations tend to have the capacity for specific architecture roles, whereas in smaller organizations, practising architecture is part of a broader role – you don't have to be an architect by title to practice architecture, but you do need the competencies (see the section 'The Competencies of a Business Architect' later in the chapter).

THE ARCHITECTURAL MATURITY OF THE ORGANIZATION

Organizations embrace business architecture relative to their architecture maturity. We discuss this further in the next section – 'Business Architecture's Position in the Organization'.

THE BELIEFS AND DESIRES OF KEY STAKEHOLDERS

These are typically, but not exclusively, the C-suite stakeholders. If there is a recognition of the need for the role, and its value can be demonstrated, then it is more likely to gain traction. The beliefs and desires of key stakeholders is also a factor in the architectural maturity of the organization.

The role can change over time, moving with the maturity of the architecture practice and the skills, competencies and experience of the business architects within it. So in different stages of the business architecture practice life cycle, different types of individuals may be required.

The lack of clear definition of the business architect's role with an organization can cause confusion and conflict. This often occurs where, for example, a business analyst undertakes the role of business architect but fails to take the broader architecture view and hence is unable to deliver the value proposition of business architecture.

Business Architecture's Position in the Organization

Business architecture is about viewing the organization as a cohesive whole, in which the individual parts and the relationship between those parts can be identified and optimized. It is about identifying problems and opportunities and formulating changes to address those problems and exploit the opportunities.

To date, the vast majority of business architecture practices reside in the IT function and report either to the CIO, CTO or another role within that function. In many cases, this is for historical reasons. Architecture as a discipline has its roots in IT infrastructure and systems. As the role extends into information and business, the problems and opportunities to be addressed are broader and have a greater impact. The fact that they reside in the IT function does not mean they are not delivering value; they may be there for a very good reason. Business architecture needs to be cognizant of the key influences that can shape and determine the behaviour, and ultimately the success, of organizations, and technology is a significant influence. In theory, business architecture should be loosely coupled from the technology such that if the technology changes, that technology can be replaced with minimal impact and exploited with positive benefits. Reality is some distance removed from that aspiration, although it is a useful architectural principle to follow.

Business architecture may exist at all levels, and the model employed should map to the operating model of the organization. Business architecture defined at the Macro level needs to permeate through the levels to ensure that projects are aligned for the value to be realized. Different segment architectures may have different operating models, although this represents a relatively complex implementation. The path of least resistance is to develop a unified model for the organization as a whole. Any progression from one architecture level to another, or from one operating model to another, should be carefully planned.

Business architecture is a discipline devoted to shaping, articulating and guiding business change and defining the optimum course between strategy and its realization. This highly collaborative role acts as catalyst and facilitator in shaping and defining the future organization with the organizational leaders and senior managers. That alone sets the role apart from any other role in the organization.

With this remit, our conclusion is that the business architecture practice should report into the Strategy function or the office of the CEO.

The Competencies of a Business Architect

The competencies of the Business Architect can determine the level within the organization at which they are able to operate.

In Table 13.1 we present some broad categories of skills and competencies that we believe are important.

Table 13.1   Skills and competencies of a business architect

Skills and Competencies	Examples
Soft	Leadership, team working, consulting, communication, negotiating, relationship management and emotional intelligence
Business	Business case development, strategic development and planning, operational risk, business continuity, innovation
Design	Modelling, systems thinking, information modelling, business process design
Change Management	Portfolio, programme and project management methods and tools
General IT Knowledge	Technology awareness and its application, information security risk

TOGAF includes an Architecture Skills Framework that defines a set of competencies (and associated proficiency levels) for various architecture roles. The framework provides:

- *'the roles within a work area;*

- *the skills required by each role;*

- *the depth of knowledge required to fulfil the role successfully.'*

Similarly, the Skills Framework for the Information Age (SFIA) 'provides a common reference model for the identification of the skills needed to develop effective Information Systems'.

Some organizations use psychometric tests to assess potential candidates as well as existing and potential practitioners within their organization. These include:

- the Myers-Briggs Type Indicator

- TDF International

- Belbin (for teams)

- proprietary tests (for example, those defined and used by management consultancies such as Social Styles)

So what are the necessary competencies required of a good business architect? The usual candidates include the hard (technical, industry, architecture methods and so on) and soft (personal, social, political and so on); today's business architect is expected to be a leader, a motivator, an innovator, a communicator, a strategic thinker, a deliverer, a politician, a diplomat, a relationship councillor, a game changer – the list goes on. Business architects are usually expected to be educated to degree level, and there is an increasing expectation that candidates will have an MBA.

Jeff Scott, formerly of Forrester, has often been asked what makes a good architect, and more often now, what makes a good business architect. He cites six competencies, as follows.

A SOUND UNDERSTANDING OF BUSINESS PRINCIPLES AND CONCEPTS

Most IT types think understanding the business is all about understanding the business processes, but this is not what business leaders are interested in. Business architects should understand how the market context affects the business, how value is created, what differentiates their company from its competitors, and how products are created, marketed, and sold. They should have a good understanding of how business strategy is developed – even if it is never articulated.

AN ABILITY TO THINK ABOUT BUSINESS PROCESSES OUTSIDE THE TECHNOLOGY CONTEXT

Even business people have a hard time with this. I have had more than one business architect share his frustration with business project people who continually talk about business processes in terms of how their applications work. Although business architects need to understand how to leverage IT for business value, they need to be able to draw a wide, heavy line between business processes and the technologies that enable them.

A REALLY STRONG CONSULTING MINDSET

Building a good business architecture is more about listening and reading between the lines than selling a concept or framework. At the end of the day, a successful business architecture will be one that resonates with business leaders. Business architects should see themselves as business consultants looking for problems to solve.

A STRATEGIC POINT OF VIEW

Business architects need the ability to challenge people's thinking, to get them out of the current issues and current systems and into thinking about the possibilities of the future. As one of my clients so eloquently put it: 'It's not so much about thinking outside the box as it is thinking outside *your* box.'

GOOD AT DESIGN THINKING

'I want business architects who can bring order out of the typical strategy chaos at most companies.' This means that they can listen to lots of ideas and create a view that resonates across the width of the organization. It means they have the ability to see what others are blind to and can create a clear line of sight between business intention and business action.

A CATALYST FOR CHANGE

At the end of the day, business architecture isn't worth the napkin it is scribbled on if the organization doesn't change. Business architects should see themselves as change agents first, and architects second. They should use business architecture as a tool to agitate and initiate action.

We also believe that for business architecture to gain traction, the business architect has to be flexible and pragmatic – happy to role-play for the benefit of the customer. That may include being able to work outside your normal mode, perhaps outside your comfort zone. The ability to adapt is critical; smaller team size means having to cover more ground – for example, if your soccer team loses a player, the remaining players have to be versatile enough to cover the ground, to cover more than one position.

Business architects need to keep an eye on trends and their implications: social networks, gamification, disruptive technologies and so on. And there are many ways to keep up to date, including attending conferences, researching, networking or training. Ultimately, there needs to be a desire to learn and understand.

Certification

Certification brings a degree of assurance that an individual meets a set of defined criteria considered necessary to fulfil the role. Certification also promotes standardization of skills within and across industries, as well as encouraging some uniformity among practitioners in terms of the definition and purpose of business architecture and greater clarity to all architecture stakeholders. This is particularly relevant in a field that is, compared to the disciplines it interacts with, in its infancy and rapidly evolving. Furthermore, the periodic renewal of certification means that practitioners keep abreast of developments – a requisite in such a fast-moving discipline.

Increasingly, organizations are requiring their existing architects to become certified, and expect new hires and consultants to be certified. It also adds to the credibility of supplier and partner organizations.

Architecture certification schemes come into existence and evolve as the discipline itself evolves. Open and proprietary certification schemes exist for the mainstream architecture frameworks (TOGAF, DODAF, FEAF, Zachman and so on), although only elements of these focus on business architecture. We are beginning to see specific business architecture certification schemes and a much closer association to MBA programmes – for example, the Business Architects Association Certified Business Architect® (CBA) scheme.[1] We also expect business architecture modules and courses to be more prevalent in higher education, and also recognized in the certification schemes of other disciplines such as MSP and PRINCE2. Like business architecture itself, business architecture certification schemes are evolving, and it is not always easy to determine which may be the most appropriate to pursue. The decision is often not a personal decision, but a corporate one that is dependent on the framework that has been selected for use.

As business architects are viewed as game-changers, leaders, communicators and so on, in addition to the harder skills (methods and techniques), an increasingly important aspect of the role is the soft skills. Although certification schemes today focus on the more technical aspects of the discipline, we would expect certification programmes to incorporate soft skills in due course. Organizations are looking for strong soft skills, and where certification is mandatory, soft skills become the differentiator between prospective candidates.

The art of being wise is the art of knowing what to overlook.
William James

---

1   See Business Architects Association, http://www.businessarchitectsassociation.org/, accessed 10 March 2012.

14

Establishing Business Architecture as a Practice

Positioning the Practice in the Organization

The architecture practice must position itself in relation to other functions, including organizational strategy, planning and change management, and solution design. Some stakeholders may question why an architecture practice is needed – after all, the organization will no doubt have a strategy function and probably a planning function, both setting direction. Faced with this kind of competition for management mind share, it is important to establish a rigorous model of how architecture will add value and how it will engage and satisfy its customers. So you must know who your customers are and how you are going to serve them. And you must have determined your differentiated proposition. What can business architects do that no one else can do?

To overcome these barriers, a clear identification of stakeholders and their needs is crucial. Firstly, for stakeholders the question is: 'How can architecture help?' Secondly, we believe that architecture should not be a sideshow at the fair: it should be the main stage, therefore a clear understanding of how and when architecture participates in the different 'change-the-business' life cycles is essential (see the sections on 'Architecture Stakeholders' in Chapter 6 and 'Life Cycles' in Chapter 7).

In support of a 'compelling value proposition' (see the Business Architecture Business Model Canvas for a business architecture practice in Appendix 3), it is worth developing a clear business mission and vision statement that demonstrates alignment and contribution towards the organization's overall vision.

Achieving the Right Balance

As somebody once said: 'You need good ingredients to make a good dish, but they also need to be combined in the right way and be served at the right time to get a great dish.' Establishing a successful practice is about composition, engagement and timing.

A business architecture capability can range from an individual functioning in a business architect role on a part-time basis to a fully funded department with tens of staff. In some cases it is appropriate to establish a business architecture practice as a formal team with an operational budget, mission and goals. In other cases it may mean undertaking some 'skunkworks' to gain traction and to grow organically. Funds and/or the lack of an executive sponsor may dictate which approach is viable; a strategy somewhere between these two may also be possible – for example, a segment-focused approach.

A business architecture practice is like a business (within a business or as an independent consultancy). As with any business, there needs to be balance between how much time is spent on set-up and ongoing refinement and how much time is spent on executing the operating model for business architecture – that is, conducting business. An inward-focused business will not generate the revenues necessary to return investment to its shareholders. A business that is poorly organized or inefficiently run will not maximize the return of investment. It will fail to satisfy demand and grow.

Achieving the right balance is critical, like growing a business; you need to make the right calls at the right time. A business architecture practice has to overcome the barriers mentioned earlier in this chapter. One way to do this is for the architects to practise what they preach and apply business architecture in establishing and running the business architecture practice itself, and in doing so, apply the engagement principles. We also recommend completing a Business Model Canvas (see Chapter 15) for the practice.

We identify the business architecture core and supporting services associated with each life cycle listed in Tables 7.7 and A.1 respectively.

Metrics should be identified and tracked for business architecture, and the same applies to the business architecture practice, although the metrics will, of course, be different. Here are some example metrics:

- customer feedback;

- number/percentage of programmes/projects assessed pre-commissioning;

- number/percentage of projects that have a Business Architecture Description (BAD);

- number/percentage of projects reviewed as compliant;

- number/percentage of architecture dispensations raised;

- number/percentage of dispensations open;

- number/percentage of time re-charged;

- number/percentage of architect re-chargeable utilization;

- number of architecture elements for each type and number of times used;

- number of architectural patterns and number of times used;

- number of areas formally supplying master data to the business architecture;

- number of staff using business architecture information each month.

In addition to the above, metrics associated with cost (for example, opportunity cost) should ideally be captured. However, this is a complex area that relies on the organization being able to monitor its benefits realization – an ability few organizations truly possess.

In large organizations there may be many architecture practices operating at different levels and/or at the same level in different segments (lines of business) or geographic locations. This may be by design, or the result of mergers or acquisitions.

Global organizations pursuing rationalization and standardization will need to employ a federated model, and that is compatible with our Four-level Business Architecture Model (with appropriate modification) – see Chapter 8.

Maturing the Practice

Improving the processes of a business should feature in every business plan, and the practice of business architecture is no exception. There are a number of models for assessing the suitability of processes and the appropriateness and reusability of the outputs from those processes, and the most widely used are based on the Software Engineering Institute's Capability Maturity Model Integration (CMMI).[1]

The general principle behind these models is a number of levels through which processes 'mature' (and a collection of measurements dimensions (practices or activities) that are relative to each level.

In architecture, most of the publicly available applications of the CMMI relate to enterprise architecture and/or IT architecture, and specifically in relation to governments and federal agencies.

For an organization in an immature state, developing standards for mature deliverables is an effective way to mature. How the deliverable is produced (that is, the process or method adopted) is less important than the quality of the deliverable produced.

An effective maturity model can help practices to assess their level maturity at a given point, and also their improvement over time; targets can be set for improvements, and plans put in place to make them happen. Using a standard maturity model enables practices to benchmark themselves against practices in other organizations. However, some maturity models are necessarily comprehensive (reflecting the context in which they are applied – for example, government practices) and would be considered heavyweight for many architecture practices. Many organizations use CMMI as a basis, and define their own measures at each maturity level. Unfortunately for some, anything less than Level 5 (Optimized) suggests that that the practice is falling short, rather than recognizing that the intention is to improve maturity. Moving

---

1   http://www.sei.cmu.edu/cmmi, accessed 10 March 2012.

from Level 2 (Managed) to 3 (Defined) in one area may be more beneficial than moving from Level 3 to 4 (Quantitatively Managed) in another area.

The two most important points to consider when addressing architecture maturity are:

1.   To make sure the purpose of measuring maturity is not lost.

2.   To make it relative to the organization.

It's not about achieving a score; it's about improving to deliver greater value. Simple measures and assessments are a good way to start.

> *Coming together is a beginning.*
> *Keeping together is progress.*
> *Working together is success.*
>
> *Henry Ford*

PART VI
Architecture Resources

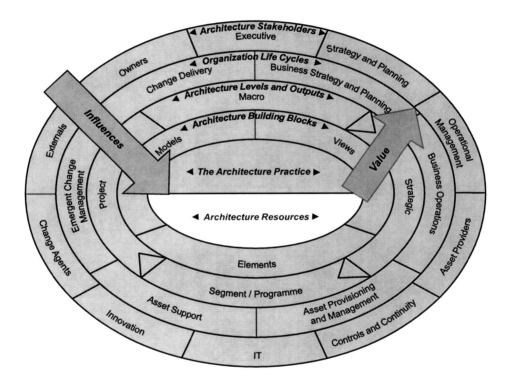

15

Architecture Frameworks

Defining Architecture Frameworks

Without our skeleton, we humans would be a heap of flesh, unable to run, jump, twist and turn as we can. The collection of bones combine to provide a highly versatile structure that supports a complex array of biological elements. It is a framework that has evolved over millions of years; it is proven, and although there may be some aspects that we would wish to change, all in all it does its job.

An architecture framework serves a similar purpose. It provides the structure on which to develop the various elements of the architecture that collectively enable the organizations to run, jump, twist and turn.

Before addressing the topic in more detail, we will define some terms so that we can draw a distinction between, for example, a 'framework' and a 'methodology'. We do this not to be pedantic, but because the differentiation is important when determining why you want to use a framework and what value you hope or expect to get from it. These definitions also give a point of reference for some of the example frameworks that we will look at later in this chapter.

Dictionary definitions[1] reveal the following:

- **Framework** – a basic structure underlying a system, concept or text.

- **Methodology** – a system of methods used in a particular area of study or activity.

- **Taxonomy** – a scheme of classification.

---

1   Oxford Dictionaries: http://oxforddictionaries.com/, accessed 10 March 2012.

ISO/IEC 42010[2] defines architecture frameworks as:

> *conventions, principles and practices for the description of architectures established within a specific domain of application and/or community of stakeholders.*

ISO/IEC 42010 also states that:

> *An architecture framework **conforms** to the International Standard (IS) when it specifies:*
>
> 1. *information identifying the framework;*
> 2. *one or more concerns;*
> 3. *one or more stakeholders having those concerns;*
> 4. *one or more architecture viewpoints (and their specifications conforming to the IS);*
> 5. *correspondence rules, integrating the viewpoints;*
> 6. *conditions on applicability;*
> 7. *consistency of the framework with the provisions of the ISO/IEC 42010 conceptual model.*

As we will see later, some so-called 'frameworks' are more methodologies than frameworks, given the definitions above. To us, the importance lies not so much in the name, structure or content of these 'frameworks', but in the value obtained from using them.

Although some existing frameworks are focused on specific industries or architecture disciplines, we do not distinguish between them in terms of the general value and pitfalls that are associated with such frameworks.

The Benefits and Limitations of Frameworks

BENEFITS

There are many benefits that frameworks can bring if they are used in the right way. They can:

---

2   ISO/IEC 42010 (originally IEEE Std 1471:2000), *Recommended Practice for Architectural Description of Software-intensive Systems,* http://www.iso-architecture.org/ieee-1471/index.html, accessed 10 March 2012.

- provide a way of classifying the elements of the architecture;

- provide a common language (or terminology) within the architecture and with the stakeholders;

- define the processes through which the architecture is described, applied, governed, measured and managed;

- promote consistency between different domains of the architecture;

- promote continuity at different levels of the architecture;

- provide an integrated approach to the development and operation of an architecture;

- promote reuse of the architecture artefacts – the intellectual property captured in the models, principles, policies, patterns and so on;

- provide a checklist for the breadth and depth of coverage of the architecture, and hence to define the scope of the organization in focus;

- promote standardization and rationalization within and outside the organization (for example, with other industry participants);

- help to determine the depth of the detail necessary to deliver the required value;

- provide a structure on which to build an architecture practice;

- improve consistency of outputs from architecture practitioners.[3]

Most frameworks provide a set of generic building blocks that enable architects to focus on those that will enable innovation, differentiation and strategic value. At the same time, these generic building blocks enable the business to draw and maintain parity with competitors in the market. The emphasis lies in the consistency between numerous organizations and change agents.

---

3   For example, engaging a TOGAF-certified architect sets a level of expectation about their knowledge of architecture.

It is easy to see how this intent can be applied within commercial organizations that live within a complex ecosystem and with large global organizations that represent microcosms of geographical spread and different organization units. However, no framework fulfils all of the above intents, as you will see when we look at a selection of frameworks later in this chapter.

LIMITATIONS

Architecture frameworks are tools, and like all tools, realizing their benefits lies in the hands of the people who use them. In other words: there are limitations to the use of frameworks. Here is a list of the most common:

- not thinking enough about your own business/situation;

- believing that frameworks must be followed rigorously;

- shoe-horning your organization into the framework;

- focusing on the framework rather than on why the framework is being used;

- adopting terminology that stakeholders do not relate to.

Many organizations fail to obtain the value they had anticipated from the adoption of frameworks. This can be attributable to the framework being used, the user of the framework, or both.

There is often a tendency to take a bottom-up approach to architecture when using a framework – focusing on defining or adapting the framework's structure (the meta model that underpins it, the set of views/viewpoints to be used, the processes to be adopted, and so on); focus is placed on the internals of the architecture rather than on the value to be generated, resulting in a lead time before any value can be realized. And when the frameworks that are used have their origins in IT, there can seem to be a disconnect between what the business is trying to achieve and what the framework is providing – it seems to be introducing some alien structure that has to be navigated. This is often a significant factor in the failure of architecture initiatives.

As we mentioned above, many frameworks have emerged from IT whose remit since birth has been to apply what computers do best: automate highly repetitive and deterministic activity. The problem with these frameworks is that they fail to assist in dealing with complex and chaotic activity that exists within organizations. The focus on supporting a living ecosystem of self-determining agents (for example, people) has only recently gained traction within IT with social networking and collaboration tools enabled through Internet technologies.

Typically, it is larger organizations that adopt (and adapt) frameworks. Some organizations even create their own frameworks, as was the case with DODAF (Department Of Defense Architecture Framework). While there tends to be a relationship between the adoption of a framework and the size of the organization, this is by no means a rule to be followed. Smaller organizations can derive great value by applying a light touch to the adoption of a framework. This can be difficult to achieve, especially when the framework itself is 'heavyweight' – comprehensive, but also complex. In this case, the skill consists of determining which elements of the framework to use, and when. Some frameworks are relatively 'light', hence the risk of over-engineering is reduced. TOGAF weighs in at almost 700 pages.

As we will see in the next section, there are a number of frameworks. No single framework is perfect – if it was, everyone would be using it. We do encourage the use of one or more frameworks. But we need to qualify that encouragement. We suggest that you:

- Take a look at the frameworks that exist – we provide a list of some of the more common ones in the next section.

- Read what people say about them and make your own judgement.

- Look to adopt (and where necessary adapt) only what you need for your immediate goals.

- Determine what value you expect to get from them.

- Use the framework, but focus on *business outcomes* – as opposed to framework outcomes.

The majority of stakeholders may not even need to know that a framework is being used. When you visit a doctor, you want a diagnosis and prognosis in lay terms; you do not need (or usually want) to know the detailed structures of anatomy, physiology or chemistry. However, it is important to remember that sponsoring stakeholders may want to know whether any recognized framework or standard is being adopted, to appreciate the risks and rewards. They may also be interested to know which of the competitors are or are not using the framework. Depending on the appetite for risk, their support may vary.

Types of Framework

In general, there are three types of framework:

1.   **Classification** – the classification of elements; providing various taxonomies.

2.   **Methodology** – describing processes and methods to establish and perform architecture.

3.   **Hybrid** – a combination of the above.

There are also frameworks that contain reference models that are specific to vertical sectors and/or generic for use across all sectors.

There are many frameworks in existence today, and there is little doubt that this number will increase, and at the same time the existing frameworks will evolve and mature; in version 2.0 of DODAF, for example, 'The major emphasis on architecture development has changed from a product-centric process to a data-centric process designed to provide decision-making data organized as information for the manager.'[4] This reflects the changing needs of its users.

Table 15.1 provides a list of the more common frameworks that relate to business architecture in some form; it is not intended to be an exhaustive list by any means. Existing frameworks evolve and new frameworks emerge, so this list is relative to a point in time. We define in the table the version and general coverage (scope) of the frameworks.

---

4   http://cio-nii.defense.gov/sites/dodaf20/background.html#whatisnew; accessed 10 March 2012.

Table 15.1   Frameworks

Framework	Description	Type*	Scope/Industry
BPTF[1]	Business Process Transformation Framework	Classification	General enterprise value chain
BTEP[2]	Business Transformation Enablement Program	Methodology	Business architecture (in the public sector)
Business Model Canvas[3]	Business Model Generation	Hybrid	Business architecture; industry independent
COBIT[4]	Control Objectives for Information and related Technology	Classification	Processes (IT)
DODAF[5]	Department of Defense Architecture Framework	Methodology	Enterprise architecture; defence-focused
FEA[6]	Federal Enterprise Architecture	Hybrid	Enterprise architecture; government-focused
Gartner[7]	EA Framework	Methodology	Enterprise architecture
GERAM[8]	Generalized Enterprise Reference Architecture and Methodology	Methodology	Enterprise integration and business process engineering
ITIL[9]	Information Technology Infrastructure Library	Methodology	Service management (IT)
MODAF[10]	Ministry of Defence Architecture Framework	Methodology	Enterprise architecture; defence-focused
NASCIO EA Tool-Kit[11]	Enterprise Architecture Development Tool-Kit	Hybrid	Enterprise architecture; government/state
PCF[12]	Process Classification Framework	Classification	Process
PEAF[13]	Pragmatic Enterprise Architecture Framework	Methodology	Enterprise architecture
SABSA[14]	Sherwood Applied Business Security Architecture	Classification	Security architecture
TOGAF[15]	The Open Group Architecture Framework	Hybrid	Enterprise architecture; industry-independent
Zachman[16]	Zachman Framework For Enterprise Architecture	Classification	Enterprise architecture; industry-independent

Notes:

* This denotes their primary focus; some methodology-based frameworks may include classification material and vice versa.

1   Business Process Transformation Framework (BPTF), http://www.value-chain.org/framework/, accessed 10 March 2012.

2   Business Transformation Enablement Program (BTEP), September 2004, http://www.collectionscanada.gc.ca/webarchives/20071125180244/http://www.tbs-sct.gc.ca/btep-pto/index_e.asp, accessed 10 March 2012.

3   A. Osterwalder and Y. Pigneur, Business Model Generation: A Handbook for Visionaries, Game Changers, and Challengers (Wiley Desktop Editions, 2010), See also http://www.businessmodelgeneration.com, accessed 10 March 2012.

4   Control Objectives for Information and related Technology (COBIT®), Version 4.1, http://www.isaca.org/Knowledge-Center/cobit, accessed 10 March 2012.

5   Department of Defense Architecture Framework (DODAF), Version 2.02, http://cio-nii.defense.gov/sites/dodaf20, accessed 10 March 2012.

6   Federal Enterprise Architecture (FEA), Version 2007, http://www.whitehouse.gov/omb/e-gov/fea, accessed 10 March 2012.

7   Gartner, Inc., http://www.gartner.com, accessed 10 March 2012.

8   Generalized Enterprise Reference Architecture and Methodology (GERAM), Version 1.6.3, http://www.cit.gu.edu.au/~bernus/taskforce/geram/versions/geram1-6-3/v1.6.3.html, accessed 10 March 2012.

9   Information Technology Infrastructure Library (ITIL®), Version 2011, http://www.itil-officialsite.com, accessed 10 March 2012.

10 Ministry of Defence Architecture Framework, Version 1.2.004 (May 2010), http://www.mod.uk/DefenceInternet/AboutDefence/WhatWeDo/InformationManagement/MODAF, accessed 10 March 2012.

11 Enterprise Architecture Development Tool-Kit, Version 3.0, http://www.nascio.org, accessed 10 March 2012.

12 Process Classification Framework by the American Productivity and Quality Center (APQC), http://www.apqc.org/process-classification-framework, accessed 10 March 2012.

13 Pragmatic Enterprise Architecture Framework, http://www.pragmaticea.com, accessed 10 March 2012.

14 Sherwood Applied Business Security Architecture (SABSA), http://www.sabsa.org, accessed 10 March 2012.

15 The Open Group Architecture Framework (TOGAF®), Version 9.1, http://www.opengroup.org/togaf, accessed 10 March 2012.

16 The Zachman Framework for Enterprise Architecture™, Version 3.0, http://www.zachman.com/, accessed 10 March 2012.

Some frameworks are 'open' – that is, their content and supporting materials (templates, guidelines and so on) are freely available with minimal restrictions on their usage – while others are proprietary. As the terms under which these frameworks are available change over time, we have not distinguished between open and closed frameworks in Table 15.1.

Many consultancies, industry analysts and architecture tools vendors also have frameworks to varying degrees. Some frameworks are industry-specific (for example, DODAF) and others are universal (for example, TOGAF).

In the next three sections we will take a brief look at three frameworks; they represent a cross-section of the frameworks listed in Table 15.1. We examine their characteristics and their applicability to business architecture. This is not an evaluation of the frameworks; it is a discussion of three very different frameworks to give you a flavour of what is available at the time of writing.

The three frameworks are:

1.   The Business Model Canvas

2.   TOGAF®

3.   The Zachman Framework for Enterprise Architecture™

As well as examining the general make-up of these frameworks, we will identify their specific relevance to business architecture.

The Business Model Canvas

The Business Model Canvas[6] is a relatively new entrant to the business architecture space. Although at its heart it has a classification framework, it also has associated processes and a variety of techniques. It is defined as being 'a shared language for describing, visualizing, assessing, and changing business models'.

The authors state that 'A Business Model describes the rationale of how an organization creates, delivers and captures value.' This is consistent with a key objective of business architecture – delivering value.

The BMC comprises nine parts, as shown in Figure 15.1.

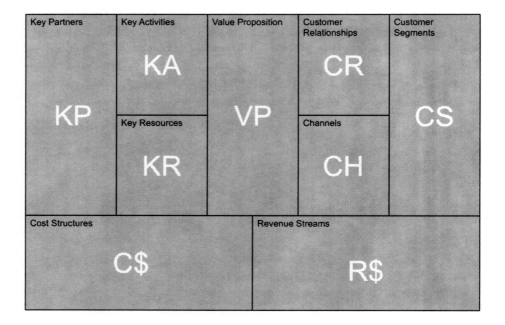

Figure 15.1   The Business Model Canvas

Source: Alexander Osterwalder and Yves Pigneur, *Business Model Generation: A Handbook for Visionaries, Game Challengers, and Challengers* (2010). Reprinted with permission of John Wiley & Sons, Inc.

CLASSIFICATION

The nine constituents of the BMC are defined as 'Building Blocks':

- The **Key Partnerships** Building Block describes the network of suppliers and partners that make the business model work.

- The **Key Activities** Building Block describes the most important things a company must do to make its business model work.

- The **Key Resources** Building Block describes the most important assets required to make a business model work.

- The **Cost Structure** describes all the costs incurred to operate a business model.

- The **Value Propositions** Building Block describes the bundle of products and services that create value for a specific Customer Segment.

- The **Customer Relationships** Building Block describes the type of relationships a company establishes with specific Customer Segments.

- The **Channels** Building Block describes how a company communicates with and reaches its Customer Segments to deliver a Value Proposition.

- The **Customer Segments** Building Block defines the different groups of people or organizations an enterprise aims to reach and serve.

- The **Revenue Streams** Building Block represents the cash a company generates from each Customer Segment (costs must be subtracted from revenues to create earnings).

The BMC has at its centre the value proposition. This balances the supply elements (partners, activities and resources) and costs with the demand elements (channels and customer relationships and segments) and revenues, as shown in Figure 15.2.

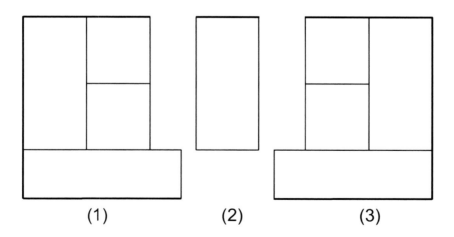

(1)   (2)   (3)

Figure 15.2   Business Model Canvas key constituents

Key:
1. Supply elements and costs
2. Value proposition
3. Demand elements and revenues

Read from left to right, the BMC represents a value chain.

The BMC recognizes that an organization can have many business models – for example, to meet the needs of different customer segments. Each customer segment may require different business activities (processes), different resources (skills), and so on. Few frameworks are explicit about this.

PROCESS

Although the focus of the framework is classification, there is an associated design process, albeit a simple one:

- *Mobilize – prepare for a successful business model design project.*

- *Understand – research and analyse elements needed for the business model design effort.*

- *Design – generate and test viable business model options, and select the best.*

- *Implement – implement the business model prototype in the field.*

- *Manage – adapt and modify the business model in response to market reaction.*

TECHNIQUES AND METHODS

The BMC is supplemented with material to help users bring their models to life – specifically, the use of scenarios to help to transition models from being abstract to reflecting a specific set of meaningful (or realistic) circumstances.

There are a number of published examples of business models documented using the BMC, and its application is agnostic in terms of industry or type of business.

Within a Strategy section, the authors recognize that strong business models are those which are developed with knowledge of the operating environment through which value is delivered – that is, they need a business architecture. There is an analysis of the external factors that constrain, inform and influence the shaping of business models; they identify four main groups: industry forces, market forces, macro-economic forces and key trends.

The BMC also includes a section on implementing business models in organizations with reference to organizational architecture, specifically designing organizations using the Star Model.[5] The Star Model proposes five elements:

- strategy

- reward systems

- organizational structure

- processes

- people

The BMC also discusses the relationship between it and enterprise architecture, in which it distinguishes between business, applications and technology architectures.

APPLICABILITY TO BUSINESS ARCHITECTURE

The BMC has a strong relationship to business architecture. Its nine Building Blocks are a useful starting point, and the high-level nature of the BMC means that it does encourage a business value focus and the delivery of value is (or at least should be) the ultimate goal of any business architecture effort. And because of the level at which it is pitched, it provides a complementary method to populate the Macro level of our Four-level Business Architecture Model (see Chapter 8).

In Appendix 3 we have completed a BMC for business architecture as a discipline. We have used this canvas to validate and demonstrate our proposition for business architects.

---

5   Summary available at http://www.jaygalbraith.com, accessed 7 April 2012.

TOGAF®

> *TOGAF[6] Version 9.1 is a detailed method and set of supporting resources for developing an Enterprise Architecture. Developed and endorsed by the membership of The Open Group's Architecture Forum, TOGAF 9.1 represents an industry consensus framework and method for Enterprise Architecture ....[7]*

The Forum comprises more than two hundred organizations globally and across a broad spectrum of industries.

TOGAF is primarily a methodology-based framework, although it also includes elements of classification, which we will discuss later.

TOGAF has been in existence since the mid-1990s, and has evolved through a number of versions to the current one.[8] Although TOGAF had its roots in IT architecture, its evolution is bringing an increasing business focus. At its heart is a development methodology that includes a business architecture phase – we will discuss this in more detail later in this section.

TOGAF comprises seven parts, as shown in Figure 15.3.

The contents of each part are described in TOGAF as follows:

- **Part I (Introduction)** – This part provides a high-level introduction to the key concepts of enterprise architecture and in particular the TOGAF approach. It contains the definitions of terms used throughout TOGAF and release notes detailing the changes between this version and the previous version of TOGAF.

- **Part II (Architecture Development Method)** – This part is the core of TOGAF. It describes the TOGAF Architecture Development Method (ADM) – a step-by-step approach to developing an enterprise architecture.

6　The Open Group Architecture Framework (TOGAF®).
7　http://www.opengroup.org/architecture/togaf/, accessed 10 March 2012.
8　Version 9.1 at the time of writing.

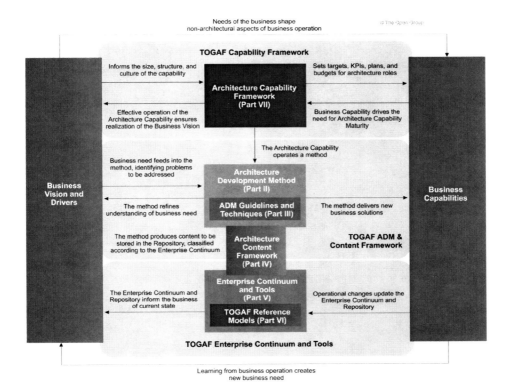

Figure 15.3   Structure of TOGAF®

© 2008 The Open Group

- **Part III (ADM Guidelines and Techniques)** – This part contains a collection of guidelines and techniques available for use in applying TOGAF and the TOGAF ADM.

- **Part IV (Architecture Content Framework)** – This part describes the TOGAF content framework, including a structured meta model for architectural artefacts, the use of re-usable architecture building blocks, and an overview of typical architecture deliverables.

- **Part V (Enterprise Continuum & Tools)** – This part discusses appropriate taxonomies and tools to categorize and store the outputs of architecture activity within an enterprise.

- **Part VI (TOGAF Reference Models)** – This part provides a selection of architectural reference models, which includes the TOGAF Foundation Architecture, and the Integrated Information Infrastructure Reference Model (III-RM).

- **Part VII (Architecture Capability Framework)** – This part discusses the organization, processes, skills, roles and responsibilities required to establish and operate an architecture practice within an enterprise.

By dividing the framework in this way, TOGAF recognizes that the parts can be used independently of the whole. One such example is a core part of TOGAF, Part II, the Application Development Method (ADM) as shown in Figure 15.4; TOGAF refers to this figure as the Architecture Development Cycle. The ADM provides an architecture life cycle divided into phases, and for each phase it sets out the objectives, approach, inputs, steps and outputs.

Central to the ADM is Requirements Management, maintaining a focus on the goal of any architecture initiative; it is the process by which architecture requirements are identified and managed.

The ADM (and TOGAF generally) does not specify:

- The level at which an architecture initiative is applied; TOGAF defines Strategic, Segment and Capability Architectures as being three levels of application. However, other levels or divisions could equally be defined such as business goal (Consistent Customer Service, Reduced Time-to-Market, etc.) business imperative (Secure Operations, Product Agility, etc.) and so on.

- The change mechanism through which any architecture initiative is progressed – for example, programme(s) or project(s).

Although on the surface the ADM implies a starting point (Phase A – Architecture Vision) and an end point (Phase H – Architecture Change Management), TOGAF recognizes that value can be obtained from applying subsets of the phases. For example, you can apply Phase B (business architecture) to establish a baseline and target business architecture and a gap analysis, and do so without completing other phases.

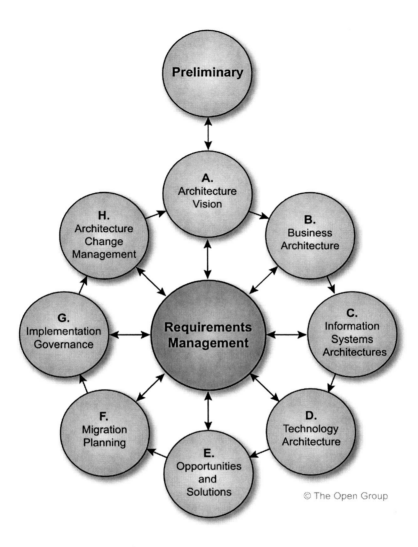

Figure 15.4 TOGAF®Architecture Development Cycle
© 2008 The Open Group

It is also possible to apply the ADM (or a subset of it) iteratively, with each iteration adding further detail to the architecture. TOGAF suggests some iteration cycles, for example a 'Transition Planning Iteration' covering Phases E and F (in which architecture roadmaps are created and refined through iteration).

TOGAF divides enterprise architecture into four 'domains': Business Architecture, Data Architecture, Application Architecture and Technology Architecture. However, other architectures could also be defined, including performance architecture, security architecture, organization architecture, each of which has a relationship to business architecture.

APPLICABILITY TO BUSINESS ARCHITECTURE

There are a number of elements of TOGAF that are applicable to business architecture, and these cover the definition, implementation and governance dimensions. Each of these can be applied specifically to business architecture, even though in some cases they may appear to have an IT focus.

Phase B of the ADM provides the focal point for business architecture; its objectives are:

- to describe the Baseline Business Architecture;

- to develop a Target Business Architecture, describing the product and/or service strategy, and the organizational, functional, process, information, and geographic aspects of the business environment, based on the business principles, business goals, and strategic drivers;

- to analyse the gaps between the Baseline and Target Business Architectures;

- to select and develop the relevant architecture viewpoints that will enable the architect to demonstrate how the stakeholder concerns are addressed in the business architecture;

- to select the relevant tools and techniques to be used in association with the selected viewpoints.

TOGAF has adopted the concept of *viewpoints* and *views* as set out in ISO/IEC 42010; 'A view is what you see; a viewpoint is where you are looking from – the vantage point or perspective that determines what you see.' The view and viewpoint of an aircraft are different for the pilot and an air traffic controller.

But it is not just Phase B that applies to business architecture. Phase A, for example, includes the creation of the Architecture Vision. At the level expected for Phase A, this equates to Levels 1 and 2 of our Four-level Business Architecture Model discussed in Chapter 8. Certainly, the abstraction of IT-related building blocks is sufficient to support the business manager's perspective of IT.

Also, in a project that involves no IT systems or technology elements, phases E (Opportunities & Solutions) to H (Architecture Change Management) still apply, as does Requirements Management.

In addition to the ADM, there are many aspects of TOGAF that, although not exclusively focused on business architecture, have a strong relationship to business architecture across the definition, implementation and governance dimensions. Appendix 4 lists the relevant TOGAF sections.

TOGAF provides a comprehensive and flexible framework that you can tailor to your own needs. However, it does not describe what the resulting architecture should look like. That is why the skill and experience of the business architect is so important.

The Zachman Framework for Enterprise Architecture™

The Zachman Framework is a structural classification of single-variable concepts. It contains descriptive representations of those single-variable concepts as normalized artefacts – that is, 'primitive models'. It is a classification-based framework – a taxonomy; it is a six-by-six matrix, as shown in Figure 15.5.

The columns represent the primitive interrogatives – What, How, When, Who, Where and Why – and the rows represent different perspectives on those interrogatives, through reification – the progressive transformation from the abstract to concrete forms. There is no order to the columns (you can put them in whatever order suits you), but there is an order to the rows, to denote the different stages that occur between scoping and realizing the operational business

Figure 15.6 provides a simplified view of the framework. In the following sections we will take a brief look at the rows, columns and cells.

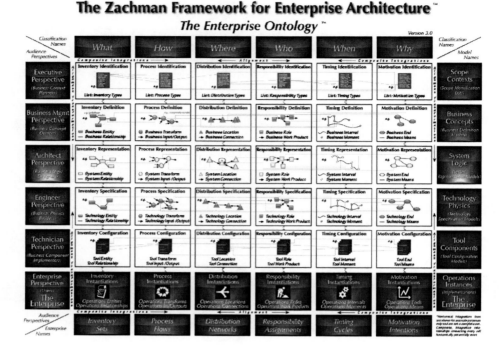

Figure 15.5   The Zachman Framework for Enterprise Architecture™

Published with the permission of John A. Zachman and Zachman International®, Inc.

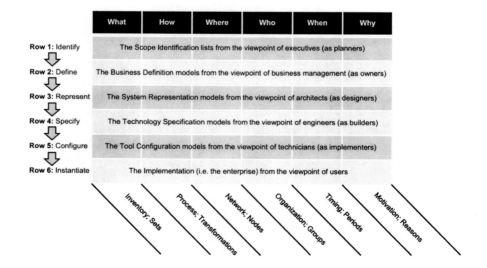

Figure 15.6   Summary of The Zachman Framework for Enterprise Architecture™

ROWS

In the Zachman Framework:

- Rows 1–2 address the 'things' the organization cares about.

- Rows 3–5 are representations of those 'things'.

- Row 6 is the organization – that is, an instantiation of the architecture.

Furthermore:

- Each of the cells in row 1 contains lists.

- Each of the cells in rows 2–6 contains models.

- Rows 1–5 address abstract models.

Therefore, there is a progression from identifying things (things that you would typically include in an inventory, such as parts, products and so on) to the representation of those things (such as data in IT systems) to the actual realization of those things in the real world. Because it includes the interrogatives, it is a way of assuring completeness (as long as nothing is lost in translation).

COLUMNS

The columns are mutually exclusive and collectively exhaustive, and unlike the rows, there is no intended order. Users of the framework will often number them to make referencing them, and more specifically the cells, easier – for example R2C3 (row 2, column 3 for the columns arranged as in Figure 15.6) for a business conceptual view of the locations of the organization. The majority of users leave the columns in the order that they appear in the published Zachman Framework.

References to 'system' and 'technology' in the Zachman Framework do not necessarily relate to 'information system' or 'information technology'.

CELLS

Each cell of the Zachman Framework contains 'primitives'. So, for example, R2C4 contains an abstraction of the roles within the organization; these could be at the level of type of organization unit (such as a sales department) and/or at an individual role level (such as VP of Sales). An actual organization chart with specific named personnel in it would be in R6C4 because it is an instantiation.

Primitives of the Zachman Framework equate to elements of the Periodic Table. Composites of the Zachman Framework are combinations of cells that have relationships between them. For example, a composite of R2C2, 'Process Definition', and R2C4, 'Organization Definition', would represent the roles that are involved in specific business processes. On any one row there are 30 uni-directional (or 15 bi-directional) possible relationships between the cells in that row. Composites equate to compounds of the Periodic Table. A common problem we find is that when people say they are finding it difficult to draw a particular diagram, more often than not when you examine the problem you can see that they are trying to combine too many of the primitives into a composite diagram. Combining cells on the same row can be difficult enough, or transforming cells from the adjacent rows of the same column, but combining cells on different rows from different columns is another matter.

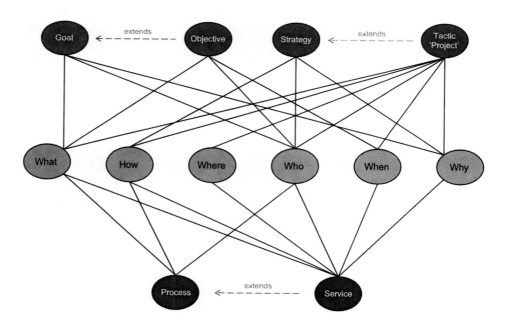

Figure 15.7   **Demonstrating composite elements using the Zachman Framework**

As we mentioned in Chapter 1, business architecture encourages the identification of the components (or building blocks) of which organizations are composed – the primitives – in the same way that a chemist identifies the elements of the Periodic Table. Once the elements are identified, the chemist can then determine the result of combining those primitive elements to form composite elements – that is chemistry. Without the knowledge of the primitives, it is not chemistry that is being practised, it is alchemy. We will look in more detail at primitives versus composites in Chapters 16 and 17 when we discuss frameworks and methods.

APPLICABILITY TO BUSINESS ARCHITECTURE

According to John Zachman, if you create and maintain the descriptive representations of your organization – that is, the primitives and the relationships between them that collectively and completely describe your organization – you will have a baseline against which you can assess, describe and manage change.

It is rows 1 and 2 of the Zachman Framework that relate to business architecture. Row 1 contains lists (of asset types – 'What'; of process types – 'How'; of location types – 'Where', and so on)

As a matrix, the Zachman Framework provides a useful classification schema. And because the Zachman Framework is a schema, it:

- does not specify the order in which any of the cells are populated, so you can define your own architecture as 'top-down', 'bottom-up' or 'inside-out';

- does not specify precisely what you put into each cell, and there is no standard for what should be in each cell;

- does not define the scope that it should cover;

- does not distinguish between current ('as is'), target ('to be'), or any intermediate states.

There are, however, some common misconceptions about the Zachman Framework, summarized in Table 15.2.

Table 15.2   Zachman Framework misconceptions

Misconceptions	Redress
You have to populate all of the cells for it to be 'complete'.	There should be no emphasis on 'completing' the framework. The emphasis should be on obtaining value from it.
The framework can only be considered to cover the enterprise if all columns are completed.	Each of the cells can have an enterprise-wide model.
The columns have a specific order.	They don't; they are independent. That said, we would usually start with the 'Why' column – which typically is the rightmost column and hence (subconsciously) is one of the last to be addressed.
The further down the rows you go, the greater the level of detail. In other words, it is a progressive decomposition from row 1 through to row 6.	Adding detail is relative to each cell, not to each row. Progression down the rows represents a transformation from one perspective to another, not more detail on the same perspective.
The Framework is a methodology.	The Framework is a classification schema; it requires a methodology to populate it.

In theory it might make sense to start with primitives and create the composites. In reality, in the organization, many of the operating elements are composites, not primitives, so you may need to extract the primitives from the composites.

The Zachman Framework is the science; the art is how to obtain the best value from it.

It is not necessary to populate the entire framework to derive value from using it. For example, by identifying the organization's process types (R2C2) and location types (R2C3) and the relationships between these process types and location types, it is possible to determine which processes are deployed at which locations – logically – and thereby determine duplication, opportunity and so on. Remember: it is R6 that contains the instantiations of those processes and locations.

Different industries will be more interested in certain columns. For example, consultancy firms that rely on the skills and knowledge of their consultants, property insurers who focus on the 'what' and 'where' of the asset they are insuring, and retailers who are concerned with 'what' inventory they have and sell.

Using Frameworks

WHICH FRAMEWORK TO USE

Which is the 'right' framework to use? The answer is: it depends. It depends on:

- the skills and experience of the architect who will populate the framework;

- the existence of frameworks already deployed within your organization (and even within partner, customer or supplier organizations);

- the resources that you have available (human and financial);

- the objective of your architecture efforts (for example, long-term versus short-term);

- the nature of your organization (for example, formal, highly structured, requiring comprehensive standards, governance and so on versus informal, agile and highly adaptive);

- the maturity of the organization in terms of business architecture.

There are consequences of immaturity. If your organization is not ready or is unable to recognize the need to improve its maturity (it may have other priorities), introduction will be more difficult. You will first have to overcome the 'not invented here' syndrome.

You may eventually decide on:

- one framework;

- a hybrid of two or more frameworks;

- no framework.

As we discussed earlier, frameworks tend to focus on the classification of architecture artefacts or the process by which those artefacts are produced. Few frameworks help to define what those artefacts should look like or provide predefined viewpoints or templates. Furthermore, real-world examples are hard to come by, as few organizations (particularly commercial organizations) want to publicize the intellectual property or unique selling proposition that may have delivered competitive advantage.

Hybrids are possible. TOGAF states that:

> As a comprehensive, open method for Enterprise Architecture, TOGAF 9.1 complements, and can be used in conjunction with, other frameworks that are more focused on specific aspects of architecture or for vertical sectors such as Government, Defense, and Finance.

We have certainly fused TOGAF with FEA and Zachman.

To illustrate: because TOGAF is method-based and the Zachman Framework is a classification schema, their complementary nature means they can be mapped to each other.[9] Another example might be using the BMC as a classification scheme for the business architecture, with TOGAF for the ADM (in particular the high-level architecture developed in Phase A). However, some frameworks are comprehensive and relatively complex: it takes experienced practitioners to combine them without being overwhelmed by the complexity.

If you use a framework, it is worthwhile investing time up-front in getting it right – not necessarily perfect, but fit for purpose. This is really what TOGAF advocates as part of the Preliminary Phase of its ADM.

There are very many cases where the use of frameworks (and more generally the use of architecture as a discipline) struggles to gain traction in organizations. The BMC is high-level, so you don't get bogged down in unnecessary detail. It encourages you to be business-driven rather than technology-driven. It is more holistic as it focuses on proposition, revenue and cost sides of the business. Also, it has not evolved from a technology framework, as the Zachman Framework and TOGAF have. It is more appealing to the C-suite than other frameworks, primarily because it is not heavyweight. Although it may be particularly appealing to smaller organizations, its simplicity can have equal appeal to larger organizations where simplicity (and clarity of thought and purpose) can be used to overcome inherent complexity.

---

9   TOGAF 8.1.1, http://pubs.opengroup.org/architecture/togaf8-doc/arch/chap39.html#tag_40_03, accessed 10 March 2012.

The BMC is, by design, top-down. The Zachman Framework and TOGAF can be either top-down or bottom-up – it depends on the objective of the architecture effort. And because the BMC is top-down, combined with its focus delivery of value, it provides a strong case where a revolutionary approach is required. TOGAF and Zachman include more detail and are well suited to a more evolutionary approach. However, as with any tool, many things are possible – it depends on the skill of the user.

One factor that may sway your adoption decision is the extent to which your candidate frameworks contain reference models relevant to your challenges. There are reference models supporting needs of a specific 'vertical' market, and reference models supporting the needs of the general or 'horizontal' market. We will discuss these in more detail in the next chapter.

Habit is habit and not to be flung out of the window by any man, but coaxed downstairs a step at a time.

Mark Twain

16

Reference Models and Architecture Patterns

What are Reference Models?

Reference models are readily available models that represent one or more aspects of a theoretical organization. They tend to be abstract in nature, hence they provide representations of real-world occurrences. Wikipedia defines a business reference model as 'a reference model, concentrating on the functional and organizational aspects of the core business of an enterprise, service organization or government agency'.[1]

Table 16.1 provides a list of the more common reference models that relate to business architecture in some form. As with the list of frameworks:

- the list is not intended to be an exhaustive;

- the models evolve and new ones emerge, so this list is relative to a point in time;

- some are 'open', others are proprietary;

- many consultancies, industry analysts and architecture tools vendors also have reference models to varying degrees;

- some are industry-specific (for example, COBIT) and others are universal (for example, BMM).

---

1   http://en.wikipedia.org/wiki/Business_Reference_Model, accessed 10 March 2012.

Table 16.1   Reference models

Reference Model	Description	Scope/Industry
ACORD[1]	Association for Cooperative Operations Research and Development	Insurance and related Financial Services
BMM[2]	Business Motivation Model	Horizontal
CBM[3]	Component Business Model; generalized models	Horizontal
COBIT[4]	Control Objectives for IT; an IT management and governance reference model	Horizontal
EM BRM[5]	Exploration and Mining Business Reference Model	Exploration, Mining, Metals and Minerals
eTOM[6]	TM Forum Business Process Framework and the broader Framework	Telecommunications
FEA Reference Models[7]	Reference models covering: Performance Reference Model (PRM) and BRM Data Reference Model (DRM) Service Component Reference Model (SRM)	Federal Government
ITIL®[8]	Information Technology Infrastructure Library	Horizontal
McKinsey 7S Framework[9]	Covers structure, strategy, systems, skills, style, staff and shared values	Horizontal
PCF	Process Classification Framework	Aerospace and defence, automotive, banking, broadcasting, consumer products, education, electric utilities, petroleum downstream, petroleum upstream, pharmaceutical, telecommunications
SABSA	Sherwood Applied Business Security Architecture	Security
SCOR®[10]	Supply Chain Operations Reference	General supply chain management
VRM[11]	Value Reference Model	Horizontal

Notes:

1   http:// www.acord.org, accessed 29 March 2012.

2   Business Motivation Model, Version 1.4, http://www.businessrulesgroup.org/bmm. shtml, accessed 10 March 2012.

3   *Component Business Models: Making Specialization Real*, IBM Institute for Business Value, http://www-935.ibm.com/services/us/imc/pdf/g510-6163-component-business-models.pdf, accessed 10 March 2012.

4   This also appears in Table 15.1, 'Frameworks'.

5   Exploration and Mining Business Reference Model, Version 1.0, July 2010, https:// www.opengroup.org/emmmv/uploads/40/22697/EM_Model_graphic_v_1.00.pdf, accessed 10 March 2012.

6   Business Process Framework (eTOM), TM Forum, http://www.tmforum.org, accessed 10 March 2012.

7   Federal Enterprise Architecture, Office of Management and Budget, http://www.whitehouse.gov/omb/e-gov/fea/, accessed 10 March 2012.

8   This also appears in Table 15.1, 'Frameworks'.

9   T.J. Peters and R.H. Waterman, *In Search of Excellence: Lessons from America's Best-run Companies* (HarperBusiness, 1982).

10   The Supply Chain Operations Reference (SCOR®), http://supply-chain.org/scor, accessed 10 March 2012.

11   The Value Reference Model, Value Chain Group, http://www.value-chain.org, accessed 10 March 2012.

Some reference models are industry-agnostic (such as BMM), and others are industry-specific (such as eTOM for the telecommunications industry). TOGAF, for example, recognizes in its Architecture Continuum that a number of levels of reference model can exist:

- Foundation Architecture

- Common Systems Architecture

- Industry Architectures

- Organization-specific Architectures

Each level of model beneath the Foundation Architecture is specialization of the model above it, so organizations may use an industry model and specialize (refine and/or extend) it to reflect their specific organization.

The Value of Reference Models

As with frameworks, reference models offer many benefits if they are used in the right way. Reference models:

- Provide a standard way of defining elements of the organization (for example, processes, capabilities, information and so on), and hence promote standardization across organization units and across architecture disciplines.

- Help to simplify the complexity of the organizational system; they are particularly valuable to large organizations striving to establish a consistent customer proposition and reduce diversity that may arise from, for example, natural entropy and business acquisition.

- Reduce time-to-market by reusing existing material.

- Help to define the scope of the organization in focus.

- Promote standardization within the organization as well as with partners, suppliers, customers and other industry participants.

- Provide a way of establishing the boundaries between elements of the organizational system.

- Help to identify duplication of capability within an organization and any variance between duplicate capabilities – this is particularly useful in the case of mergers and acquisitions.

- Provide a good architecture communication vehicle.

- Provide a structure for decomposition to more granular levels.

- Support a holistic view of the organization.

Many organizations are striving for global standardization, but without creating globally agreed and understood points of reference (or 'reference models'), implementation of such strategies can only be hindered.

In summary: reference models allow organizations to easily (and cost-effectively) adopt best practice in areas of the business that do not generate strategic value. This leaves more time to concentrate on areas that will deliver competitive advantage and strategic value. There is no sound reason why an organization wouldn't want to adopt open standards in this way. Sooner or later, maintaining proprietary capability that is already commoditized in the marketplace makes no commercial sense: it will become a major impediment to the organization.

In the same way that reference models have similar benefits to frameworks, they also have similar limitations; here is a list of the most common:

- not thinking enough about your own business/situation;

- believing that reference models must be followed rigorously;

- shoe-horning your organizational system into the reference model;

- focusing on the reference model rather than on why the reference model is being used;

- adopting terminology that stakeholders do not relate to.

Despite these limitations, reference models represent an important tool in the business architect's tool bag.

Architecture Patterns

Patterns have their origins in the architecture of buildings (and specifically the work of Christopher Alexander[2]), where it was recognized that different projects incorporated many of the same problems, and that generic solutions could be applied to similar problems.

In its most general sense, a pattern is a recurring form or arrangement of elements. It is the result of experience of having solved the same problem many times (and learnt from the shortcomings of earlier solutions), and so provides a solution to a known problem. A pattern is a solution to a problem that exists in a specific context. The solution has been tried and tested and is the most appropriate solution to the problem in that context. A pattern can be compared to a cookie-cutter or a playbook used in sports like American football to describe offensive and defensive play tactics.

Patterns have an important role to play in society – in the architecture of buildings, mathematics, statistics, geometry, language, process and methods – and business patterns can be found wherever reuse of design is sought.

A pattern captures the information necessary to apply design successfully on a repeated and rapid basis. Well-documented patterns describe: intent and the problem being solved, motivation, applicability and limitation, participants and their responsibilities, how the pattern solves the problem, related patterns, along with an example. A pattern can describe structure and behaviour.

---

2   C. Alexander, *A Pattern Language: Towns, Buildings, Construction* (Oxford University Press, 1977), and C. Alexander, *The Timeless Way of Building* (Oxford University Press, 1979).

Structural patterns describe how resources within the ecosystem are assembled or configured. Examples of structural patterns include:

- part–subassembly

- subassembly–assembly

- assembly–product

- contract

- value chain

- process chain

Behaviour patterns describe how elements within the ecosystem collaborate, or how elements change over a period of time. Examples of behaviour patterns include:

- supplier–broker–client

- plan–do–check–act

- observe–orient–decide–act

- the Pareto principle (or 80:20 rule)

- statistical distributions – for example, normal

The real value of patterns is that they capture and codify know-how so that it can be referenced, reapplied, modified and evolved many times over. Patterns require discipline to develop and document, but once they are developed and tested, they become packages of wisdom that are even patentable.

> *It is the mark of an educated mind to be able to entertain a thought without accepting it.*
>
> *Aristotle*

17

Architecture Tools, Meta Models and Standards

The Role of Architecture Tools

In Chapter 1 we discussed the structure of the organization that is comprised of a complex set of elements and associations between those elements. Also, there are the architecture views and viewpoints of the numerous stakeholders to capture and furnish in the business architecture. The larger the organization and the architecture effort, the more intricate the job of defining, maintaining, optimizing, communicating and managing the architecture and all its facets.

Like organizations, architecture tools are evolving to address ever-increasing needs to:

- understand the enterprise in term of the components of which it is comprised and the relationships between those components;

- enrich the view of the 'enterprise':

    - to include the wider ecosystem of suppliers, partners and so on, and
    - to create 'line of sight' from business vision and strategic objectives through to the investments made in each of the business and technology capabilities.

- assess the impact of change events – such as regulatory changes, competitor activity, disruptive technology emergence and so on;

- plan organizational change.

There are few tools whose primary focus is business architecture. From the perspective of the tool vendors, business architecture is typically viewed as being a part of a broader enterprise architecture – often defining specific elements as relating to business architecture (for example, Business Processes, Organization Units, Roles, Functions, Information Entities and so on). Therefore, we will refer to enterprise architecture tools from this point on.

Using Tools for Business Architecture Outputs

There are a number of ways to capture and construct a business architecture description. Normal office tools such as word processors, spreadsheets, diagram/drawing tools, Mind Mapping™ and presentation software provide a cost-effective, starter solution; self-adhesive labels and whiteboards provide an excellent medium during workshop and concept development to gather input data. These tools provide a quick and easy way to start, and certainly office documents provide an accessible medium into which a BAD can be placed and upon which formal change control can be applied.

Ease of use, accessibility and cost are major advantages for these office tools. However, there are a number of major drawbacks associated with the use of office documents as the sole medium or source of business architecture information over the longer term, such as these:

- Office documents contain non-structured information and information that is not inter-connected or related in a way that allows reuse. In a small-scale or relatively static situation, this does not represent a major problem. However, in large organizations these features only serve to hinder business architects. They also make maintenance of the architecture almost cost-prohibitive.

- Office documents create islands of information. As soon as information needs to be represented in multiple documents or multiple chapters within a document, duplication and redundancy of information is created – and so is the overhead required to maintain parity across the duplication.

- Office documents cannot be computer-validated or computer-verified. It is therefore difficult (and expensive) to enforce a level of rigour and quality control to ensure consistency in a large architecture practice and over time. If architecture sits at the thin edge of the wedge, small discrepancies, contradictions or inaccuracies will lead to much large problems further down the line during implementation of the architecture (at the thick end of the wedge).

- Sharing office documents and allowing multiple architects to work on the development of a business architecture is impractical. Such an approach prevents creation of a scalable architecture practice and elongates timelines for delivery.

One step up the maturity curve is defining standards and creating templates. While this can improve the quality of BADs, it does not solve the fundamental problems outlined above.

Business architects working in more mature environments use tools that go beyond the capability of a template one might have experienced in a word processor. They use tools with a relational database (or repository), and unlike a word processor template that allows the user to amend it, these multi-user tools ensure that the architect captures the architecture in prescribed ways that can be automatically validated and verified using predefined rules.

With these repository-based tools, an architect can develop each necessary view of the architecture using prescribed rules, and then, when ready, can manually or automatically aggregate them together into a BAD (office) document and place them under change control for review, sign-off and subsequent publication and communication. Architecture information will be shared across multiple views, and the adoption of modelling tools based on relational database technology means that information is stored only once, even though it appears in different forms in different places.

Tooling is useful in a static situation, but really comes into its own when the business architecture is under development and fluid. During this time, without such tooling much time can be wasted maintaining duplicated data in the architecture. Using a modelling tool, the architecture information can be captured once and then reused many times without the overheads of duplication. In other words: it gives the architecture information economies of scope.

The most advanced organizations are using these tools as a means to automatically configure workflow and business process management software without human (programmer) intervention. Using these tools and business process automation platforms, organizations are beginning to massively reduce the *concept-to-benefits realization* change life cycle.

This all sounds great, as these tools only capture information once, so the productivity of business architects improves dramatically. However, with all upsides there are usually downsides. These tools, though powerful, require investment and struggle to match the aesthetic quality that might be achieved using a standard desktop presentation tool. Many have poor abilities to hide detail information contained within the architecture and can be slow during conceptualization when everything is potentially fluid. Some output appears too 'raw' or too complex for management consumption. It may be more cost-effective to create presentation alternatives for major decision points within the change life cycle, knowing that the duplication created will not create an excessive overhead.

Finally, if business architects are to maintain a description of the business, they must remember they are tracking a moving target. Gaining access to up-to-date information and keeping it up to date is a challenge. It requires stakeholders to commit to supply information on an operational basis. For that to happen, business architects must provide some reciprocal value in return, otherwise, inevitably when budgets are tight, the supply of data will cease. The only way to resolve this motivational issue is to provide informational tools that can help the data suppliers.

Architecture Tool Features

Enterprise architecture tools exist to support the growing demand to manage the complexity of architecture. Figure 17.1 represents the feature sets necessary in a modern-day tool.

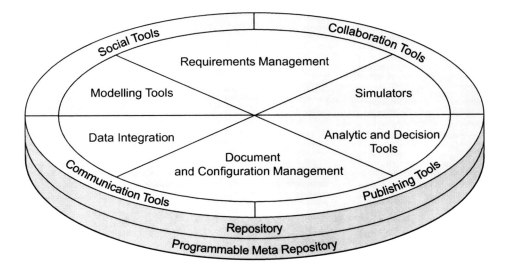

Figure 17.1   Architecture tool feature sets

Enterprise architect tools exist to support the architecture, but the architecture exists to support the organization, so it must be possible to trace from the use of the tool to the vision, goals and objectives of the organization. The definition of an appropriate meta model and resultant stakeholder views and viewpoints should all be established to support the vision, goals and objectives of the organization.

The architecture meta model gives the specification required to structure (or program) the tool. Because of this programmability, enterprise architecture tools currently represent the most viable option.

Today, the core features of enterprise architecture tools include:

- a repository to store and manage architecture elements and the relationships between them;

- an architecture meta model to structure the architecture artefacts;

- one or more methods/frameworks (support for the Zachman Framework, TOGAF and so on);

- models, matrices and other views of the architecture elements and their relationships (for example, views for processes, locations, organization).

Emerging features include:

- optimization/rationalization

- simulation

- risk analysis

- impact analysis

- cost analysis

- value analysis

We expect to see continuing product development, including greater integration with tools used by other disciplines such as portfolio, programme and project management.

Selecting a Tool

The development and evolution of architecture tools is fast-moving. There are sources that periodically evaluate the latest offerings, such as the annual assessments from industry analysts Forrester[1] and Gartner.[2]

The selection of an architecture tool should follow the same process as the selection of any other business tool (application, system, service, infrastructure and so on).

There is no tool that is right for every organization; you need to determine your specific (known) needs and map those to the features and functions of the tool. There are likely to be several enterprise architecture tools that are suitable

---

1   *The Forrester Wave™: Enterprise Architecture Management Suites*, published by Forrester Research, Inc., http://www.forrester.com, accessed 10 March 2012.
2   *Magic Quadrant for Enterprise Architecture Tools™*, published by Gartner Inc., http://www. gartner.com, accessed 10 March 2012.

for an organization's needs; choice is ultimately determined by factors other than features and functions – such as cost, licensing and training needs.

As with business architecture itself, the use of an architecture tool should focus on the value you aim to get from it. For example, typical core goals of the organization might be:

- revenue protection and growth

- cost control and reduction

- improved agility

- brand and reputation

- customer service and satisfaction

- employee satisfaction

- regulatory compliance

- operational excellence

- environmental awareness

So the question is: how will a tool help me to fulfil these goals? One way of answering this question is to determine what views and viewpoints you will need (underpinned by a complementary meta model), and then use those in the evaluation process.

Benefits and Limitations of Architecture Tools

At the time of writing, the most widely used tools for enterprise architecture are office desktop tools that already exist within the enterprise, and they are readily available at no additional cost. For many organizations, they are adequate.

And of course, there are the flipchart and whiteboard, and pen and paper in a one-to-one discussion. Sometimes the 'features' of automated tools can constrain the unencumbered thinking of the architect (or any other user of the tool); the high degree of interaction of a whiteboard session can be invaluable, not just for communication, but for relationship-building and for establishing common mental models.

It is possible to acquire architecture tools too early in the architecture practice life cycle. We have experienced situations where the early focus of the architecture effort is influenced by the capabilities of the tool rather than the goals of the architecture practice. So there is a balance to be drawn. However, as the architecture practice matures, the need for a specialist tool becomes increasingly apparent.

Regardless of the maturity of the practice, one problem that will remain is how to gather and maintain up-to-date information. This challenge grows the more 'current state' views are maintained, as tracking a moving target requires operational processes to keep the data accurate. This problem is compounded as you maintain lower-level architectural information. To motivate information contributors, you will need to ensure you provide more valuable information in return.

Architecture Meta Models

META MODELS

An architecture meta model, or metadata model, is a model of the architecture's data (or entities – the things the architecture needs to model) and the relationships between them. Probably the best way to describe a meta model is to use an example. A dictionary is a meta model of the language that we use day by day. A more complex example is TOGAF's meta model, shown in Figure 17.2. It identifies those entities that relate to business architecture – that is, TOGAF's definition of business architecture – and their relationship to entities in other TOGAF architectures (data architecture, application architecture and technology architecture).

Each entity is defined along with its relationship to other entities. The model forms the foundation of architecture modelling, so it is important that it is well thought out. Extending it is easier than changing it, so it is worthwhile to invest some initial time defining your key entities and relationships. Refer back to Chapter 10, which outlines the contents of an extensive business architecture meta model.

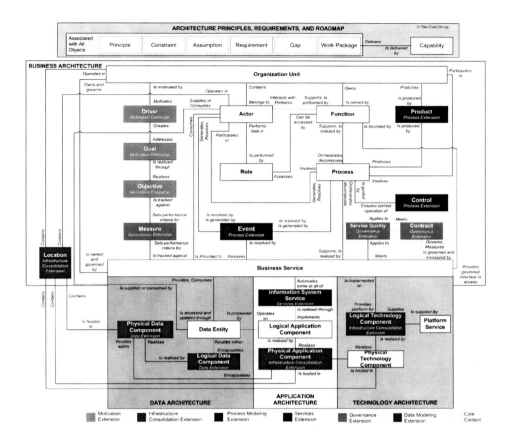

Figure 17.2   Relationships between entities in the full TOGAF® meta model
© 2008 The Open Group

The value of a meta model is that it:

- defines the underlying structure of the architecture;

- provides the 'raw materials' for the development of architecture assets;

- provides a formal way to link (and hence provide traceability between) related architectures;

- provides a common language on which the architecture can be assembled.

With respect to the last point, the entities in the meta model represent the basic or most granular elements from which architecture perspectives can be taken. TOGAF 9 suggests some common viewpoints and views specifically for business architecture, including (but not limited to):

- catalogues:

    - organization/actor catalogue
    - driver/goal/objective catalogue
    - role catalogue
    - business service/function catalogue
    - location catalogue
    - process/event/control/product catalogue
    - contract/measure catalogue

- matrices:

    - business interaction matrix
    - actor/role matrix

- core diagrams:

    - business footprint diagram
    - business service/information diagram
    - functional decomposition diagram
    - product life cycle diagram

- extension diagrams:

    - goal/objective/service diagram
    - use-case diagram
    - organization decomposition diagram
    - process flow diagram
    - event diagram

Because an architecture meta model defines the underlying structure of the architecture, it is important that it is thought through, especially if the architecture initiative is to stand the test of time and significant architecture assets are to be based on it. For example, it needs to be extensible so that if a new concept is introduced to the organization – such as a new product category or channel to market – there is no impact on the existing model other than perhaps to extend it.

You can create your own meta model from scratch by using our model in Chapter 10, or by using an existing framework meta model or one of the meta models that accompany architecture tools.

HOW MODELS AND META MODELS ARE USED IN THE DEVELOPMENT OF BUSINESS ARCHITECTURE

The overriding need to model is predicated by the fact that to scrap and rework the models of your business is more costly and slower than models that are maintained progressively, hopefully before each change in the business takes effect.

The second predicate is the fact that to enable the first predicate, a level of rigour must be introduced as an enabler.

The third predicate is to help introduce a common language with common semantics that everyone in the business can use to discuss, design and describe the architecture.

The fourth predicate is that bringing the information together in one place can generate immense value through aggregation and combination in the same way a data warehouse does.

Chapters 10 and 11 show the different types of information used to describe a business, and the ways that information can be combined can create a significant information management problem unless specialist tools are used. Secondly, it is up to each organization to determine which specific kinds of building block will be most useful in describing its business. So any solution enabling the capture of this information and/or the construction of models should be configurable to meet the organization's needs.

To allow the tooling to be configured, the normal route is to construct a model about the information needed to construct business architecture (models), otherwise known as a meta model. With this meta model built, it can be used to configure the tooling and thus allow the tooling to model only what is required by the users. Obviously, changes to the meta model will be required as the business architecture practice evolves. Such changes can be used to reconfigure the tooling and alter the way business architecture models can be constructed.

Architecture Standards

It would seem reasonable to assume that there are architecture standards defined to support architecture development. However, at the time of writing there are surprisingly few. This seems counterintuitive given that the key resources of business architecture include frameworks and reference models. Standardization of these elements should make a positive contribution to the business architecture value proposition.

Business processes, functions, organization units, locations, capabilities, roles and so on are fundamental constituents of the organization; it is their existence and the way that they interact that determines its 'character'. However, there is no common, standard way of representing these constituents. Although some specific standards exist, such as the Business Process Model and Notation[3] language for process modelling and the Unified Modelling Language[4] (UML) for systems engineering, those standards focus on specific elements rather than the relationships between elements.

One attempt to fill the gap is Archimate®,[5] which is a vendor-independent enterprise architect technical standard adopted by the OpenGroup and appearing increasingly in vendor tool offerings. Archimate has a Business Layer (with an associated Business Layer Meta Model) that 'offers products and services to external customers, which are realized in the organization by business processes performed by business actors'. As an enterprise architecture standard, Archimate attempts to provide a mechanism for traceability between architecture domains.

> *An architect's most useful tools are an eraser at the drafting board, and a wrecking bar at the site.*
> *Frank Lloyd Wright*

3　*The Business Process Model and Notation (BPMN), Version 2.0*, published by OMG, http://www.omg.org/spec/BPMN/2.0/, accessed 10 March 2012.

4　*The Unified Modelling Language™ (UML), Version 2.0*, published by OMG, http://www.uml.org/, accessed 10 March 2012.

5　*ArchiMate® 1.0 Specification*, published by The OpenGroup, http://www.opengroup.org/archimate/doc/ts_archimate/, accessed 10 March 2012.

18

The Future of Business Architecture

Business architecture is at level 1 in terms of its maturity. From organization to organization, the underlying methodology is generally undocumented, deliverables are not standardized, and the definition of what a business architect's roles and responsibilities are is variable. It was for these reasons that we embarked on this practical guide – as a means to help consolidate at level 1 of maturity before moving on to level 2.

In time, the world will emerge from financial crisis and nations and economies will return to an even keel. Disruption will continue to occur as a consequence of new business models and new technologies, so the demand for business architecture will grow.

Over the coming years, business architecture practices will evolve their value proposition and establish differentiation, delineation and integration with other practices and disciplines. The answer to the question 'How can business architecture help business strategy and planning?' will become clearer, as will the answer to the question 'How does business architecture relate to portfolio, programme and project management?'

Recognition of what business architecture is capable of, outside its current small community, will grow. Consultancy firms who are undertaking business architecture for their clients will do so explicitly under the flag of business architecture. And we expect that the business architecture practice will escape the predominant grasp of the IT department and move up the food chain, closer to the CEO and the Strategy function. We believe it will also build closer ties with innovation functions.

The concepts and language of business architecture continue to mature. As business architecture practices learn to overcome the current barriers, experience of 'in-the-field' engagement will create the feedback required to learn and evolve ad hoc methods into repeatable methods. The role of the business architect, still emerging in the eyes of executives and senior management, will crystallize and grow in importance.

Increasing demand will fuel improved tooling and information repositories (currently confined to a modelling resource), and will evolve into a business analytics and decision-making information warehouse – a warehouse focused on change-the-business activity rather the run-the-business which is the current offering from data warehouses. Having said this, the two worlds may collide, and that may also involve master data management and enterprise resource planning system information as well.

If we look at current market activity, there are numerous communities of interest focused on evolving business architecture – but they are fragmented. Bodies of knowledge are being established; business architect 'professions' are being created and differentiated from business analysts and other kinds of architect. Certification schemes are also emerging, and there are standards claiming to address business architecture – albeit partially, in our view. Information technology and service companies are pushing hard, for their increasingly sophisticated customer propositions are becoming more dependent on well-defined and robust business architectures. Therefore, business architectures will be defined not on paper or in presentations, but in repositories that can be linked and integrated with technology design repositories. The numerous concepts we outlined in Chapter 10 will serve to drive and refine business design for those business areas heavily dependent on technology and those that need to respond to market conditions and opportunities with agility.

With all this activity, you might think that evolution will be smooth and rapid. There is, however, a problem: IT-oriented organizations and individuals with an IT bias are driving this activity. These groups are involved in open development of standards, bodies of knowledge and professions, but there is little end-user organization participation. The absence of non-technology-sector Fortune 1000 business representation in all of this activity is stark. There are opportunities here for management consultancy firms, business schools and business associations.

We believe that to make real progress in the evolution of business architecture, a sea change is required. Documented breakthroughs using business architecture that demonstrate it publicly as a strategic weapon will need to surface. Real-world case studies and tried-and-tested patterns of how business architecture can be applied need to emerge. At the moment, business architecture has a buzz and it is probably peaking in hype. Only when it becomes a topic of strategic importance in prominent publications will it grab the headlines and attention of non-IT-oriented organizations and professionals. But we could be wrong; the non-competitive environment of government could provide a breeding ground for success and documented case studies that could cross over into the private sector arena. Truly open-source projects may push the boundaries as well.

Whichever route is taken, a step change will occur, we just don't know when.

The pessimist sees difficulty in every opportunity. The optimist sees the opportunity in every difficulty.
                                        Sir Winston Churchill

Appendix 1:
Business Architecture
Supporting Activities

Table A.1 shows the business architecture supporting activities that are associated with each of the life cycles.

Table A.1   Business architecture supporting activities by life cycle

Life Cycle Groups	Life Cycles	Business Architecture Supporting Activities														
		Strategic Planning Support	Tactical Planning Support	Operational Planning Support	Communication Management	Stakeholder Engagement	Configuration Management	Environment and Tooling Management	Financial Management	Information Management	Quality Management	Performance Management	Resource Management	Risk Management*	Service Management	Supplier Management
Business Strategy and Planning	Strategic Planning	◆	◆		◆	◆			◆	◆			◆	◆		◆
	Medium-term Planning	◆	◆		◆	◆			◆	◆			◆	◆		◆
	Annual Budget Planning	◆	◆		◆	◆			◆				◆			
	Rolling Forecast Planning	◆	◆		◆	◆			◆				◆			
	Performance Balanced Scorecard	◆	◆	◆	◆	◆			◆	◆	◆	◆	◆	◆		
	Change Portfolio Management		◆	◆	◆	◆			◆	◆	◆		◆	◆		

Life Cycle Groups	Life Cycles	Strategic Planning Support	Tactical Planning Support	Operational Planning Support	Communication Management	Stakeholder Engagement	Configuration Management	Environment and Tooling Management	Financial Management	Information Management	Quality Management	Performance Management	Resource Management	Risk Management*	Service Management	Supplier Management
Change Delivery	Programme		◆	◆	◆	◆			◆	◆	◆			◆		
Change Delivery	Project			◆	◆	◆			◆	◆	◆			◆		
Emergent Change Management	Continuous Improvement	◆	◆	◆	◆	◆	◆	◆	◆	◆	◆	◆	◆	◆	◆	◆
Emergent Change Management	Business Innovation	◆	◆	◆	◆	◆			◆	◆	◆	◆	◆	◆	◆	◆
Emergent Change Management	Technology Innovation	◆	◆	◆	◆	◆		◆	◆	◆	◆	◆	◆	◆	◆	◆

Business Architecture Supporting Activities

Business Architecture Supporting Activities

Life Cycle Groups	Life Cycles	Strategic Planning Support	Tactical Planning Support	Operational Planning Support	Communication Management	Stakeholder Engagement	Configuration Management	Environment and Tooling Management	Financial Management	Information Management	Quality Management	Performance Management	Resource Management	Risk Management*	Service Management	Supplier Management
Business Operations	Operations			◆	◆	◆								◆		
	Operational Test and Learn			◆	◆	◆										
	Operational Campaign			◆	◆	◆										
Asset Provisioning and Management	Asset Portfolio Management	◆	◆	◆	◆	◆			◆	◆	◆	◆		◆	◆	◆
	Change Management	◆	◆	◆	◆	◆	◆				◆	◆		◆	◆	
	Release Management				◆	◆	◆							◆	◆	

Business Architecture Supporting Activities

Life Cycle Groups	Life Cycles	Strategic Planning Support	Tactical Planning Support	Operational Planning Support	Communication Management	Stakeholder Engagement	Configuration Management	Environment and Tooling Management	Financial Management	Information Management	Quality Management	Performance Management	Resource Management	Risk Management*	Service Management	Supplier Management
Asset Provisioning and Management	Monitor and Control			◆	◆	◆					◆	◆		◆	◆	
	Architecture	◆	◆	◆	◆	◆	◆	◆	◆	◆	◆	◆	◆	◆	◆	◆
	Acquisition				◆	◆		◆	◆	◆	◆	◆		◆	◆	◆
Asset Support	Incident Management				◆	◆					◆	◆			◆	
	Problem Management				◆	◆					◆	◆			◆	
	Event Management				◆	◆					◆	◆			◆	

Life Cycle Groups	Life Cycles	Business Architecture Supporting Activities														
		Strategic Planning Support	Tactical Planning Support	Operational Planning Support	Communication Management	Stakeholder Engagement	Configuration Management	Environment and Tooling Management	Financial Management	Information Management	Quality Management	Performance Management	Resource Management	Risk Management*	Service Management	Supplier Management
Asset Support	Request Management				◆	◆					◆	◆			◆	
	Service Fulfilment				◆	◆					◆	◆		◆	◆	

Note:

* This covers Operational Risk and Systemic Risk.

Appendix 2:
Viewpoint Template

Presented below is what we consider essential information with which to catalogue each viewpoint:

- unique reference

- name

- intent

- business architecture level: macro/strategic/programme/project

- stakeholder(s)

- stakeholder concern(s) – framed as questions to be answered using the viewpoint:

  – for target architecture
  – for current architecture

- format: narrative/table/matrix/diagram/chart/picture

- notation: specify any formal notation or key to be used

- answer content:

  – kinds of architecture element presented
  – kinds of relationship between each element presented

 - the attributes of each kind of element
 - the attributes of each kind of relationship

- examples – capture to illustrate (people learn better by example)

- viewpoint family

- timeline – current/interim/target.

Taking the last two items, 'viewpoint family' and 'timeline' are worth discussing as you are likely to find viewpoints come in 'clusters' or 'families'. Without these classifications, one may find oneself creating very long names for these viewpoints and struggling to manage them. For example: a process view at the *Strategic level* architecture may present value streams; the 'same' view at the *Segment/programme level* may present processes; the 'same' view again at the *Project level* may present processes and sub-processes using a BPMN notation. One may use the SIPOC[1] view also. These variants of the same viewpoint can be clustered under the same viewpoint family as they all related to process, but they serve different stakeholders and provide different levels of detail.

Another reason for these families arising is that one may find that at a specific level in the architecture, for the same stakeholder, one may wish to present different information depending on the timeline being presented. Sponsors are usually more interested in the detail of a target process than the current process; they are also less inclined to invest in documenting a process that is about to be replaced. Therefore, the detail of the target process view, for example, may be different to the current architecture equivalent. 'With timeline' viewpoints can be classified and grouped together by the timeline they serve.

---

1   SIPOC is a Six Sigma tool used to present a view of a process with its suppliers, inputs, outputs and customers.

Appendix 3:
Business Architecture Business
Model Canvas

As a part of our work on this book, we completed a BMC for a business architecture practice – see Figure A.1.

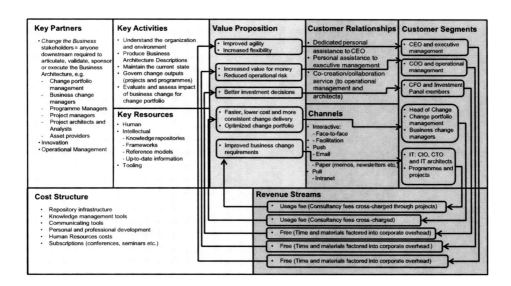

Figure A.1   Business Model Canvas for a business architecture practice

As there are a number of customer segments, we have aligned the value proposition with specific customer segments, customer segments with the revenue streams, and revenue streams back to the value proposition to ensure complete traceability.

Note, however, that some stakeholders may play dual roles: for example, function/business line heads may also be partners and customers.

Appendix 4:
TOGAF® Applicability to Business Architecture

Table A.2 lists those sections of TOGAF® that have a strong relationship to business architecture.

Table A.2   TOGAF® applicability to business architecture

		Content Relevant to Business Architecture
PART I	Introduction	Introduction Core Concepts Definitions
PART II	Architecture Development Method	Primarily phases: Preliminary, A, B, E, F, G, H and Requirements Management, in particular Phase B
PART III	ADM Guidelines and Techniques	Architecture Principles Stakeholder Management The Concept of Business Scenarios Gap Analysis Business Transformation Readiness Assessment Risk Management Capability-based Planning
PART IV	Architecture Content Framework	The (Architecture) Content Meta Model Architectural Artefacts Architecture Deliverables Building Blocks
PART V	Enterprise Continuum and Tools	Enterprise Continuum Architecture Partitioning Architecture Repository Tools for Architecture Development
PART VI	TOGAF Reference Models	Not directly relevant

		Content Relevant to Business Architecture
PART VII	Architecture Capability Framework	Establishing an Architecture Capability Architecture Board Architecture Compliance Architecture Contracts Architecture Governance Architecture Maturity Models Architecture Skills Framework
	Appendices	Supplementary Definitions Glossary

Glossary

Where appropriate, we have used existing definitions and noted the sources in parentheses.

Agent A kind of architecture *element*. Agents are used to represent parts of the architecture that may be described as active, initiative, non-deterministic, self-minded, chaotic, natural, social or organic (usually reserved for people, organization units and organizational entities).

Architecture The fundamental organization of a system, embodied in its components, their relationships to each other and to the environment, and the principles guiding its design and evolution (The Institute of Electrical and Electronics Engineers, IEEE).

Architecture Framework A foundational structure, or set of structures, which can be used for developing a broad range of different architectures. It should contain a method for designing an information system in terms of a set of building blocks, and for showing how the building blocks fit together. It should contain a set of tools and provide a common vocabulary. It should also include a list of recommended standards and compliant products that can be used to implement the building blocks (TOGAF).

Artefact See Deliverable.

Asset Any kind of non-consumable or financial resource on which the organization is reliant for its success.

Blueprint   A type of business architecture description used to describe the organization. Typically, a blueprint is associated with descriptions that depict the higher levels of the architecture. In particular, MSP uses the term to describe programme-level architecture. Blueprints depict how the building blocks and agents found within a business fit and operate together, rather than any classification of these elements often depicted in reference models.

Building Block   A type of architecture element that is usually passive, reactive, deterministic, synthetic or technological.

Represents a (potentially re-usable) component of business, IT or architectural capability that can be combined with other building blocks to deliver architectures and solutions (TOGAF).

Business Architect   A role associated with the execution of business architecture activities.

A person undertaking the role of business architect.

Business Architecture   A blueprint of the enterprise that provides a common understanding of the organization and is used to align strategic objectives and tactical demands (The Business Architecture Special Interest Group).

The business strategy, governance, organization and key business processes information, as well as the interaction between these concepts (TOGAF).

A part of an enterprise architecture related to architectural organization of business, and the documents and diagrams that describe that architectural organization. Business architecture bridges between the enterprise business model of an enterprise or a business unit on one side and the business operations that implement the business architecture on another side (Wikipedia).

Business Architecture Description (BAD)	A deliverable that takes the form of narrative, tables, matrices, diagrams, charts and pictures to represent the business architecture, or aspects of it.

Since business architecture is often modelled, narrative gives way to more visual forms of representation over narrative. Information is presented through a series of views aimed at addressing one or more concerns of a specific stakeholder. |
| **Business Case** | The justification for an organizational activity (strategic, programme, project, operational) which typically contains costs, benefits, risks and timescales and against which continuing viability is tested (MSP). |
| **Business Model** | The rationale for how an organization creates, delivers and captures value (Business Model Generation).

A broad range of informal and formal descriptions to represent core aspects of a business, including purpose, offerings, strategies, infrastructure, organizational structures, trading practices, and operational processes and policies (Wikipedia). |
| **Business Process** | See Process. |
| **Capability** | An ability that an organization, person or system possesses to do something or achieve certain outcomes. Capabilities are typically expressed in general and high-level terms, and require a combination of organization, people, processes, systems and technology to achieve: for example, marketing, customer contact or outbound telemarketing. |
| **Componentization** | An outcome sought to enable flexibility and inter-operability. A componentized solution is easier to integrate and also easier to progressively change and upgrade over time, building block by building block or component by component.

See also Encapsulation. |

Composite (Element or Building Block)   An assembly of architectural elements.

Critical Success Factor (CSF)   An element that is vital for a strategy (or tactic) to be successful.

C-suite   The group of executive management roles, including CEO, CFO, COO, CIO and CTO.

Deliverable   An output from a business architecture activity.

Domain   A specified sphere of activity or knowledge (OED).

TOGAF identifies four architecture domains: business, data, application and technology.

Element   Any discrete item that could be used to describe a business within the architecture.

A generic term used to describe an *agent*, a *relationship* or a *building block*. See the definitions for these terms.

Encapsulation   A quality achieved through design to enable componentization of building blocks. Encapsulation is achieved through the creation of 'black boxes', where the internal mechanics and composition of the building blocks are deliberately hidden from those who consume them. This allows the internals of the building blocks to change or the building blocks to be substituted by newer versions without necessarily impacting the consumer.

See also Componentization.

Enterprise   The highest level (typically) of the description of an organization, typically covering all missions and functions (TOGAF). An enterprise will often span multiple organizations.

Enterprise Architect	A role associated with the execution of enterprise architecture activities.
	A person undertaking the role of enterprise architect.
Enterprise Architecture	The fundamental organization of a system embodied in its components, their relationships to each other and to the environment, and the principles guiding its design and evolution (IEEE Standard 1471-2000).
	A formal description of a system, or a detailed plan of the system at component level, to guide its implementation (ISO/IEC 42010:2007).
Framework	See Architecture Framework.
Goal	A statement about a state or condition of the enterprise to be brought about or sustained through appropriate means (BMM). A goal amplifies a vision – it indicates what must be satisfied on a continuing basis to effectively attain the vision.
Governance	The discipline of monitoring, managing and steering a business (or IS/IT landscape) to deliver the business outcome required (TOGAF).
Interface	A means to interact with a component or building block. Discrete interfaces are used to enable encapsulation. For example, the electric wall socket and plug of an electrical device conform to a predefined interface standard: the electrical current is fixed, as are the shape and configuration of the pins of the plug and socket, to prevent misuse and ensure safety in use.
Key Performance Indicator (KPI)	A financial or non-financial metric used to help an organization define and measure progress towards organizational goals (and objectives).

Layering	A specific technique used in componentization to create a separation or isolation barrier between one set of components and another.
	For example, a Single Point of Contact (SPOC) employed within a call centre creates a layer between the call centre operatives and the customers. Within this layer, the routing logic for calls can be optimized (even dynamically), independent of the customer and call centre operatives. Equally, resources within the call centre can be increased, decreased or balanced based on type of call without impacting the customer.
	See also Componentization.
Lean	A production practice that considers the expenditure of resources for any goal other than the creation of value for the end customer to be wasteful, and thus a target for elimination. Working from the perspective of the customer who consumes a product or service, "value" is defined as any action or process that a customer would be willing to pay for (Wikipedia).
Life Cycle	The series of changes in the life of an element from its conception to its cessation.
Managing Successful Programmes® (MSP)	A methodology developed by the Office of Government Commerce to standardize programme management practices across UK government.
Meta Model	A model of a model, or a meta-description of a model, serving in the same way that a dictionary provides definitions for the words used in language. A meta model can be extended and be used to constrain the model it describes in the same way that rules for grammar define how the different types of words can be combined in the construction of a sentence.

Mission   The ongoing operational activity of the enterprise (BMM). Its definition should be broad enough to cover all strategies and the complete area of operations.

Model   A representation of a subject of interest (TOGAF). A model provides a smaller-scale, simplified and/or abstract representation of the subject matter. A model is constructed as a 'means to an end'. In the context of enterprise architecture, the subject matter is a whole or part of the enterprise, and the end is the ability to construct views that address the concerns of particular stakeholders – their viewpoints in relation to the subject matter.

Modularization   Synonymous with Componentization.

Objective   A statement of an attainable, time-targeted and measurable target that the enterprise seeks to meet in order to achieve its goals (BMM).

Operating Leverage   A measurement of the degree to which a firm or project incurs a combination of fixed and variable costs.

Operating Model The abstract representation of how an organization operates across process, organization and technology domains in order to deliver value defined by the organization in scope (Wikipedia).

Opportunity Cost The cost of an alternative that must be forgone in order to pursue a certain action (Investopedia). Put another way: the benefits you could have received by taking an alternative action.

Organization   A social group which distributes tasks for a collective goal (Wikipedia).

There are a variety of legal types of organizations, including corporations, governments, non-governmental organizations, international organizations, armed forces, charities, not-for-profit corporations, partnerships, co-operatives and universities.

Organization Unit

A real internal unit within an organization: for example, teams, departments, divisions, subsidiaries and branches. An organization unit may be a legal entity within a group of companies. An organization unit is a type of agent.

Organizational Entity

An organization set up as a legal entity.

Pattern

A solution to a problem that exists in a specific context. This solution will have been tried and tested and is the most appropriate solution for the problem in that context.

Policy

Policies enable the realization of the architecture principles by providing specific rules with which all architectural initiatives should comply.

Portfolio

All the programmes and stand-alone projects being undertaken by an organization, a group of organizations or an organization unit (MSP).

Primitive (Element or Building Block)

A basic (atomic or unitary) element of the architecture of a known class or kind.

(Architecture) Principle

A qualitative statement of intent that should be met by the architecture (TOGAF). It has at least a supporting rationale and a measure of importance.

Process

A set of activities, methods and practices that transforms a set of inputs into a set of products and services (BPMM).

Programme

A temporary, flexible organization structure created to co-ordinate, direct and oversee the implementation of a set of related projects and activities in order to deliver outcomes and benefits related to an organization's strategic objectives (MSP). A programme is likely to have a life cycle that spans several years.

Programme   The co-ordinated organization, direction and
Management   implementation of a dossier of projects and transformation
                       activities (the programme) to achieve outcomes and realize
                       benefits of strategic importance (MSP).

Project   A management environment that is created for the purpose
                       of delivering one or more business products that results in
                       a required change of state of the operating organization
                       according to a specified business case (PRINCE2).

                       A temporary organization that is created for the purpose
                       of delivering one or more business outputs according to a
                       specified business case (MSP).

RACI and RASCI   Alternate titles for a technique used to define accountabilities
                       and responsibilities within an organization: Responsible,
                       Accountable, Supporting, Consulted, Informed.

                       A full explanation is provided by Wikipedia.[1]

Reference Model   An abstract framework for understanding significant
                       relationships among the entities of an environment, and for
                       the development of consistent standards or specifications
                       supporting that environment (TOGAF).

Relationship   A type of architecture element that represents associations
                       between other architecture elements. For example,
                       relationships between building blocks and agents may
                       include: causality, dependency, location, applicability,
                       ownership, command/control, composition, inheritance, or
                       any other meaningful and useful associations.

Roadmap   A plan for change that usually spans business cycles and
                       which includes a series of progressive states. A roadmap
                       can be defined at numerous levels: organization, product,
                       capability and so on.

Segment   The architecture of an element of an organization.
Architecture

---

1   http://en.wikipedia.org/wiki/Responsibility_assignment_matrix, accessed 10 March 2012.

SIPOC   A Six Sigma tool used to present a view of a process with its suppliers, inputs, outputs and customers.

Six Sigma   A business management strategy originally developed by Motorola, USA in 1986. Six Sigma seeks to improve the quality of process outputs by identifying and removing the causes of defects (errors) and minimizing variability in manufacturing and business processes (Wikipedia).

Strategy   A course of action that is an element of a plan devised through the science and art of business leadership exercised to ensure the most advantageous conditions (BMM).

Stretch Target   A very aggressive or challenging goal (or objective if measurable).

Tactic   A course of action that is a device or expedient to be employed as part of a strategy (BMM). Compared to a strategy, a tactic tends to be shorter-term and narrower in scope.

Taxation   Any kind of direct tax, indirect tax, custom, levy, excise or tariff that may be subject to payment or reclaim by an organization.

TOGAF®   A detailed method and set of supporting resources for developing an enterprise architecture (TOGAF). Developed and endorsed by the membership of The Open Group's Architecture Forum, TOGAF® 9 represents an industry consensus framework and method for enterprise architecture.

Value Chain   A value chain disaggregates a firm into its strategically relevant activities in order to understand the behaviour of costs and the existing and potential sources of differentiation (Porter). A firm gains competitive advantage by performing these strategic activities more cheaply or better than its competitors.

Value Network   A perspective that describes social and technical resources within and between businesses (Wikipedia). The nodes in a value network represent people (or roles). The nodes are connected by interactions that represent tangible and intangible deliverables. These deliverables take the form of knowledge or other intangibles and/or financial value. Value networks exhibit interdependence. They account for the overall worth of products and services. Companies have both internal and external value networks.

Value Stream   An end-to-end collection of activities that creates a result for a customer.

View   A specific set of architectural information to a standard dictated by the template of the viewpoint (ISO 42010).

See also Viewpoint.

Viewpoint   A viewpoint describes the stakeholder (user), the concern addressed by the view (the content), and other things such as format and style (ISO 42010).

A viewpoint is like a lens or filter that you can use to view the architecture. Each different architecture or part of the architecture you observe through the lens will give a different view.

See also View.

Virtuous Cycle   A virtuous circle or a vicious circle (also referred to as virtuous cycle or vicious cycle) is a complex set of events that reinforces itself through a feedback loop (Wikipedia). A virtuous circle has favourable results, and a vicious circle has detrimental results. A virtuous circle can transform into a vicious circle if eventual negative feedback is ignored.

Vision   A description of the future state of the enterprise, without regard to how it is to be achieved (BMM).

Zachman
Framework™

The Zachman Framework™ is a schema: the intersection between two historical classifications that have been in use for literally thousands of years (Zachman International). The first is the fundamentals of communication found in the primitive interrogatives: What, How, When, Who, Where and Why. It is the integration of answers to these questions that enables the comprehensive, composite description of complex ideas. The second is derived from reification, the transformation of an abstract idea into an instantiation that was initially postulated by ancient Greek philosophers and is labelled in the Zachman Framework™: Identification, Definition, Representation, Specification, Configuration and Instantiation.

Index

Page numbers in **bold** refer to figures and tables. BA in subentries denotes Business Architecture.

Game Theory in Management
Modelling Business Decisions and their Consequences
Michael Hatfield
Hardback: 978-1-4094-4241-7
Ebook: 978-1-4094-4242-4

Enterprise 2.0
How Social Software Will Change the Future of Work
Niall Cook
Hardback: 978-0-566-08800-1

Smart Working
Creating the Next Wave
Anne Marie McEwan
Hardback: 978-1-4094-0456-9
Ebook: 978-1-4094-0457-6

The Culture Builders
Leadership Strategies for Employee Performance
Jane Sparrow
Paperback: 978-1-4094-3724-6
Ebook: 978-1-4094-3725-3

Visit **www.gowerpublishing.com** and

- search the entire catalogue of Gower books in print
- order titles online at 10% discount
- take advantage of special offers
- sign up for our monthly e-mail update service
- download free sample chapters from all recent titles
- download or order our catalogue